Three Men in Two Canoes

Three Men in Two Canoes

by

Roger Annable
Roger 'Jim' Murton
David Hudson

2019

FENNEL'S PRIORY LIMITED

Published by Fennel's Priory Limited

www.fennelspriory.com

First published in 2019

Copyright © Roger Annable,
Roger Murton, David Hudson

R Annable, RJ Murton and DA Hudson have asserted their right under the Copyright, Designs and Patents Act 1988 to be identified as the authors of this work.

All rights reserved. No part of this publication may be reproduced, stored in a retrieval system or transmitted, in any form or by any means, electronic, mechanical, photocopying, recording or otherwise, without the prior permission of Fennel's Priory Limited.

A CIP catalogue record for this book
is available from the British Library.

ISBN 978-1-909947-68-9

Designed and typeset in 12pt Bembo.

Produced in England by Fennel's Priory Limited.

The epic 1967 canoeing adventure down the River Wye, across the Severn Estuary, along the Gloucester and Sharpness Ship Canal, up the River Severn to Stourport and by canal to Kidderminster. 180 miles travelled by three novice canoeists in leaking, canvas-covered, wooden-framed kayaks.

Contents

Preparing for the Adventure

St. Peter's College and the Saltley Factor 1
The Challenge is Set 7
A Plan Unfolds 9
Information about the Waters 13
Equipment and Provisions 21
All Go, 'Come What May' 27

The Adventure

Day 1: Travel to Glasbury, Making Camp 31
Day 2: Glasbury to Bredwardine 39
Day 3: Bredwardine to Camp Inn above Hereford 49
Day 4: Camp Inn to Fownhope 59
Day 5: Fownhope to Ross-on-Wye 69
Day 6: Ross-on-Wye to Symonds Yat 75
Day 7: Symonds Yat to Tintern 83
Day 8: Tintern to Chepstow 91
Day 9: Chepstow to Purton Bridges (Severn Estuary). 103
Day 10: Purton Bridges to Wainlode 121
Day 11: Wainlode to Ketch Hotel below Worcester 129
Day 12: Ketch Hotel to Kidderminster 135

Post-adventure

Return to College 147
Post-Saltley Reunions 153
The 50th Anniversary Reunion 165

About the Three Men

Roger Annable 173
Roger 'Jim' Murton 185
David Hudson 197

"P.E. students were required to undertake an adventure journey from which they returned full of strange tales."
R.D.H. Seaman, Vice-Principal, St. Peter's College, Saltley, Birmingham, 1953-1976

"Not only was this expedition a magnificent achievement it was also the most outstanding of all those it was my pleasure to supervise. As for Health & Safety and Risk Assessment? Just don't go there!"
Steve Allatt, P.E. Tutor, St. Peter's College, Saltley, Birmingham, 1962-1972

"For you to have known Captain Billy Groves was brilliant."
James Hewitt, founding member of the Severn Area Rescue Association (SARA), May 2017

"Your expedition was unique at its time and probably remains so. It makes grand reading!"
Mervyn P Fleming, Commander SARA, Beachley Lifeboat Station, 2017

Editor's Notes

The original handwritten account of this 180-mile canoeing journey down the River Wye, across the Severn Estuary, along the Gloucester and Sharpness Canal, up the River Severn to Stourport and then by canal to Kidderminster, has been in my care since leaving our three-year teaching training course at St. Peter's College, Saltley, Birmingham in July 1967.

The account, which we referred to as 'The Log', was the daily record of a 12-day canoeing adventure that – as 21-year-old Physical Education students – Rog, Jim and I had submitted to our college tutors for assessment of our outdoor activities ability. I had always hoped to make copies of it for my two companions, but time passed and I lost contact with Rog and Jim in the early Seventies.

The log was mothballed in my attic with other college manuscripts and memorabilia. It remained forgotten for over 40 years until I decided to de-clutter the loft and rediscovered it. What an amazing revelation it was; even my colour photographic slides had survived the years. It was obvious to me that the log was a record of a monumental achievement, unique in its time, and almost certainly never completed by anyone since. My conscience dictated that I must transcribe the log and somehow find Rog and Jim to reunite them with the original account. Hopefully Jim would still have his colour slides and Rog his cine film of our expedition; together the material might make interesting viewing for others.

The process has been an incredible journey: transcribing the log, finding my friends, and rediscovering the images of the adventure has renewed friendships and brought us back into contact with people who witnessed our adventure fifty years ago. I feel privileged to present this account of our expedition and subsequent reunions.

This book, which we have entitled *Three Men in Two Canoes*, is our legacy. It will appeal to those who seek adventure. We hope that you will appreciate the simplicity and courage of our enterprise all those years ago, and marvel at its success. For we were successful. We were young men driven by pure challenge, out to prove what could be achieved when strength and determination are combined with the bonds of friendship and good humour. As we said in the college report that followed our expedition: "We staked our lives on a power that can never be built into an engine – the extra strength that men can always find within themselves when they know they must." Our adventure proved that human spirit can overcome great obstacles, great distances, and even time itself.

180 miles, 50 years, three men and two canoes. This is our story.

David Hudson
Kinver, South Staffordshire, April 2019

Preface

In 1967, three intrepid young college men from Saltley College, Birmingham, embarked upon a canoeing adventure that was to become a first. Roger Annable, David Hudson and Roger 'Jim' Murton travelled 180 miles in twelve days, traversing two great rivers, a ship canal, and one of the most dangerous tidal estuaries in Great Britain. They battled fearsome and life-threatening currents in basic, leaking, canvas canoes. And all with virtually no canoeing experience. Ignorance, to them, was bliss; but they had blind faith and often mistaken confidence in their abilities. Why did they do it? They wanted to do something worthwhile that had not been done before, which would prove their physical strength and stamina as part of their studies to become P.E. teachers.

The route was drawn by hand and the adventure captured as a daily log supported by colour photographs and cine film. All of this was protected during their journey in plastic bags stowed into their leaking canoes. It has survived to this day and is included within this book.

Whilst many canoeists complete various segments of the journey today, especially the 100-mile Glasbury to Chepstow – Hay to Monmouth – Monmouth to Tintern and Chepstow to Beachley routes, SARA (the Severn Area Rescue Association) has rarely been advised of any canoeist making safe passage across the Severn Estuary from Beachley to Sharpness.

This 1967 adventure, as captured here, is unique.

Preparing for the Adventure

St. Peter's College and the Saltley Factor

Saltley Church of England College for Teacher Training, latterly known as St Peter's College, was originally the Worcester, Lichfield & Hereford Diocesan Training College. It was built in open countryside in 1852 around a quadrangle in the Tudor style of an Oxford college and housed just thirty male students.

The traditions and ethos of St Peter's were masculine and many believed it would be a mistake to depart from this. However, by the mid-1960s, the demand to increase the total number of students above 300 meant this position could not be sustained. The first women were admitted as day students in September 1966 and as residents in 1967. All were welcomed and enjoyed the friendliness and ethos of the Saltley community, known as the 'Saltley Factor'.

It is remarkable* how well the Physical Education course maintained its popularity in the 1960s. There was never difficulty in filling the course and the College owed some debt to the P.E. Department for exceeding its quota on occasions when it was proving hard to reach the total numbers required in other subjects. Saltley P.E. students and teachers seemed to have no difficulty in obtaining jobs and deserved the splendid reputation that they enjoyed in the West Midlands.

From its origins in the leafy suburbs of the 1850s, the college had been overtaken by the urban expansion of Birmingham. By the 1960s it had become an 'inner ring' environment and perhaps not high on the list of student choices. Many of the college buildings and its facilities hardly matched up to the newer colleges that developed post-war. The college fought hard to protect its status, but St. Peter's College – aka Saltley College – closed in 1978.

Much can be said about the specialist Physical Education Course at St. Peters in the 1960s, all on limited 'postage stamp' facilities in urban Birmingham. It offered an all-round coverage of gymnastics, movement, dance, sports and games with an emphasis on how to teach. The qualification at the end would enable graduates to teach in schools with fully-equipped gymnasia. Three staff ran the course with about twenty students in each first, second and third year of the course. The Department was headed up by Jack Osborne, otherwise known as 'The Major'. He was a softly spoken gentleman who set the context, theory, and history of Physical Education & the Olympic Movement along with Child Development. The Major had been a student at Saltley and had dominated life there since World War II. He was strongly devoted to the College and to the P.E. course which he had run for so long. He deplored injustice and supported the freedom of others to speak their mind. He also had a lovely sense of humour. He became part of Saltley folklore when, following frequent sniggers whenever he mentioned 'balls' in lectures, he said "Gentlemen when I say balls I mean 'balls'. If I mean testicles I will say so!" The Major assumed seniority over the evergreen Bill Middleton, also known as 'Blackjack', a dour character who was seemingly there first, even before the war, and offered expertise in Swimming, Life Saving ("Have you got your Bronze?") and Anatomy & Physiology. Bill was never without his round-framed National Health Service spectacles. (He seemed obsessed to repeatedly tell students of the poison from infected teeth travelling to the site of old injuries and causing further inflammation and pain.) The third member of staff was the young Steve Allatt, freshly out of teaching in Birmingham and with whom most students closely related. It was he who introduced the Expedition Project into the course, having completed his as part of his Diploma at Carnegie College, and so he assumed responsibility for it.

All three staff encouraged the students, insisting on a meticulous and analytical approach to planning and teaching. Students learned to teach through practical experience and guidance on Instructional Teaching Practice, confident that they would be a good teacher whatever the circumstances. If one could teach in Inner City Birmingham (within the Number 8 bus route) as students did often on Teaching Practice, then one could teach anywhere. Saltley had been turning out good teachers for many years and seemingly every Head Teacher in the city was an 'Old Salt'. There was a certain fostering of pride in being at Saltley and a feeling within the P.E. students that we were the best.

The students' pride was reinforced by the outstanding record of College sports' teams, and their very talented players in years 1964-67 (when the three authors were studying). In almost every sport, particularly rugby, cricket and football, Saltley students made their mark★.

★ *The book 'St. Peter's College Saltley 1944-1978', written by R.D.H. Seaman, M.A. (Oxon), Vice-Principal of Saltley College from 1953 until 1976, reports that Saltley student John Woodford had a successful cricket career with Yorkshire; John Mason and John Cocking played football at international amateur level for England while still at the College, then on leaving college Mason played professionally for*

Peterborough and Cocking went to America and developed soccer there with Phil Woosnam; Howard Riley was Leicester City's outside right in the 1963 cup final and played for the college mid-week; '64-67 was the period when the Corless brothers, Barrie and Trevor, were at College. Barrie was Saltley's only International Rugby Cap and his brother obtained an International Trial. Barrie played for England against Australia in 1975 and again for England in all the home international matches in 1977 and 1978. In Athletics David A Hudson (one of the three authors of this book) competed in the High Jump at the 1965 English Indoor Athletics Championships at RAF Cosford.

The three authors were born in the 1940s and then had a classic '1950s upbringing'. But, 'the times they were-a-changing'. The authors were part of a new generation challenging every aspect of the 'Can't Do Society'. They'd been inspired by the film *The Conquest of Everest* in 1953 and were quick to embrace 1960s culture. Clothes and fashion were rapidly changing, although most days were spent in College tracksuits. Evenings were different. In 1964 everyone packed into the College Bar on Thursday evenings to follow the new music of the Beatles and the Rolling Stones broadcast on a small black-and-white television. Wednesday evenings were also spent in the bar, analysing games played that afternoon. Discussions and banter were fuelled by Newcastle Brown ale and enthusiastic singing of rugby songs with very rude lyrics, especially if teams had won (which they usually had).

The week's activities built towards Saturday (lectures in the morning) with important matches in the afternoon and dances on Saturday evenings. Bigger and better bands were being booked and such names as the Mighty Avengers, the Move and the Zombies were popular acts at Big Beat Nights.

The college bar only served drinks on Wednesday, Thursday

and Saturday, hence visits to the nearby 'Country Girl' public house on other evenings. There the authors would tackle the pub's enormous cheese butties while enjoying a shandy in the smoky atmosphere. Morning visits to the College Café were often required, to get a sausage sandwich and play the pinball machine, especially when the authors had overslept and missed breakfast.

Confidence was high following England's 1966 football World Cup victory, but half of the College seemed to be Welsh. They let everyone know that rugby was their sport, and that this was 'their time'; leading very soon to the classic 'Gareth Edwards and Barry John' Wales Triple Crown Champions era. There was a sense of 'limitless potential' in what the students could achieve. By 1967 the authors' P.E. Group were all qualified F.A. Coaches, Football Referees, AAA Coaches, and MCC Coaches. All they needed was 'the challenge to end all challenges' to prove that they were ready to graduate. Like Edmund Hillary and Tenzing Norgay in 1953, they needed their 'Everest' to prove that things, previously thought impossible, could actually be done. Their challenge was waiting, not in the shape of mountaineering equipment but in the form of two canoes.

The Challenge is Set

February 1967, Friday 9.15am, P.E. Lecture Room, Saltley College, Birmingham

The three authors and 15 other Third Year Physical Education students were seated early. The Head of the P.E. Department, known as 'The Major', entered the room. Steve Allatt, one of the three P.E. tutors, accompanied him. The Major walked calmly and confidently to the front and addressed the all-male class: "Gentlemen," he said, with a nasal snort, "Good Morning". The class replied with a cheerful and respectful "Morning!" their affection reflecting The Major's pride and devotion to his students and their achievements.

The Major told the group about John Fellows and Eric Ricketts, students from 1955-57, who had sought adventure outside the college P.E. course. They had canoed along the canal from Saltley Gasworks to Solihull, which seemed to be a journey from 'the ridiculous to the sublime'. The Major asked Steve Allatt to explain how this adventure initiative had been developed to become an assessed outdoor activity part of the P.E. course.

Steve told the students that he underwent a similar exercise at Carnegie College, finding it to be both testing and enjoyable. He'd suggested to Major Osborne that it might be included as a new assessed part of the Saltley P.E. syllabus. The Major had agreed, so it was now Steve's pleasure to supervise the Expedition

Adventures. He stressed there were many previous ventures of which the participants could be justly proud; and hopefully still gave them joy in their recollections of their involvement. He thought a snippet of one of the previous adventures might amuse us, so regaled us with a story from January of 1963. "It was the coldest night of the century," he began, "when a group of three, including former senior Saltley student Bob Knight, decided to defy the odds and camp out in the Peak District. One of the party, named Whitehead, very bravely started the next day by taking a dip in a stream bordering the field. Alas, he succumbed to the cold and it was necessary for Knight to apply artificial respiration – bottle to mouth method – to revive him. I'd have been tempted to mark the report highly on that incident alone, but unfortunately the overall standard precluded any such subterfuge. Instead, I'm now seeking for you to plan and undertake an expedition adventure that will impress me. You can complete it during the first week of the Summer Term; any longer would clash with the Easter vacation. So long as you camp out on at least one night, you have an 'open canvas' – pun intended – for your adventure. You can go anywhere in the UK, individually, as a pair, or a small group. The college will loan equipment to you but offer no financial support."

Steve sat down and the Major spoke: "Well, there you are gentlemen. We have set the challenge. Now it is down to you. We will require a written diary of your daily activities. If you participate as a pair or a group, then one account will be acceptable. The most important thing is for you to have an *adventure*. Plan for it and *enjoy* it!"

A Plan Unfolds

Following the Major's and Steve's talk, Dave and Jim met in Rog's study bedroom in Lyttleton House, the most modern of the Saltley student accommodation. It was light, spacious and comfortable; very different to the basic 'cells' that Dave and Jim had lived in during their first two years at college and less 'hairy' than their current lodgings with an elderly widow and her moulting dog 'Chummy'.

Discussions began quickly about the challenge set by the P.E. staff. The three would-be adventurers talked of their experiences the previous year at Plas Gwynant Outdoor Activities Centre in Snowdonia, where they had spent a week doing a preliminary mountain leadership course. This had been excellent training for life in the mountains: walking, basic rock climbing and abseiling, camping, route-finding and safety procedures. Every P.E. student had written their individual account of the course, some taking photographs to illustrate their participation, and Rog had astounded everyone by producing a new cine camera to record the events of the week. Sadly, foul weather meant that canoeing was cancelled. Disappointed by the cancellation, Dave decided to purchase a canoe. After some investigation he secured a second-hand PBK 20 double kayak designed by Percy Blandford – a well-known canoeist and author of the book *Canoeing Waters*. This canvas-covered touring kayak was fifteen-foot long, had a 32-inch beam, and could carry 600lb. A fine vessel, but a double canoe needed a partner to help paddle it. In August that year, Dave had persuaded Jim to help him launch the kayak.

Neither Dave or Jim had canoed before, but they managed to convince Dave's father that it would be 'no problem' and therefore secured his assistance in transporting them by car to Welshpool on the River Severn. They were dropped off with the canoe and enough camping equipment for their four-day trip back downriver to Stourport, where Dave's dad would collect them and bring them home. No written or photographic record was made of the journey, but they completed it without capsizing or having to demonstrate their advanced swimming skills.

Proud of their success, Dave and Jim discussed the possibility for another, but longer, canoe trip for their college adventure. Perhaps voyaging further down the Severn? Or maybe a coastal experience around the Isle of Wight? They could consult Blandford's guide to canoeing waters and refer to their road map of the British Isles for inspiration.

There would be advantages of cost and convenience if the planned route started and finished at Dave's home in Kinver, South Staffordshire. If Dave's dad was willing, it would be possible to transport their canoe to the upper River Wye at Glasbury, 60 miles to the west, then canoe down the river to Chepstow, cross the Severn Estuary to Sharpness, canoe up the ship canal to Gloucester, paddle up the Severn to Stourport and then by canal to Kinver. An estimated 180 miles by canoe. The more they considered it, the more they liked it. The decision was made. This would be their adventure.

And then a problem arose. Rog, who had been listening patiently, asked if he could come with them. Dave and Jim were stunned. They frowned, thinking "Two's company, three's a

A Plan Unfolds

crowd". But Rog was their friend and they didn't want to dismiss his request too abruptly. They put forward their reservations: "You have no experience," they said, "you don't have a canoe – or any camping equipment." Roger seemed unperturbed. In desperation, Dave said, "Wouldn't you be happier doing something on your own?" The ploy didn't work. Roger was confident in his response: "Yes I've never canoed before, but neither had you until briefly last year. Besides, I'm a quick learner and could pick up the techniques 'as I go', which is just what you'd done. I could borrow a single canoe and camping equipment from the College," and then, pausing for effect, said: "guys, I *really value* your friendship. Surely you wouldn't want to go without me? Oh, and don't forget, I have a cine camera and could film the adventure."

Dave looked at Jim; Jim looked at Dave. Without a word they nodded. It was a done deal. Rog was going with them. "You're in," they said.

The adventure would now be 'three men in two canoes'.

Information about the Waters

In 1967, the best available guide to canoeing in the British Isles was written by Percy W Blandford. It was entitled *Canoeing Waters* and published by Lutterworth Press. Fortunately, Dave had purchased a copy before he and Jim ventured down the Severn. They found the descriptions of their route to be concise and very helpful. Blandford's book was now referred to for advice on new waters to be included in the itinerary. (Also consulted were British Waterways' booklets: *The Severn Waterway and The Staffs and Worcs Canal*; *A Chart of the Navigable Reaches of the River Severn and the Gloucester and Berkeley Canal* published by P. Alun Jones; *The Wye Valley in Colour*, a Cotman Colour Book; and various Ordnance Survey maps.) The following information was gleaned:

River Wye

"In the popular part below Glasbury there are simple rapids at intervals, and there is enough of interest to occupy a canoeist of moderate experience for a week. The scenery is good and the water is clean. It is a natural river, with no man-made weirs or other obstructions. It is unlikely portages will be necessary, although there may be some places where wading is unavoidable. There is a right of way from Hay to the sea. In fact there have been no objections to canoeing from Glasbury."

"The distance from Glasbury to Chepstow is 100 miles.

The tide almost reaches Bigsweir Bridge, which is about 6 miles downriver of Monmouth. This is part of the Bristol Channel tide (the second highest in the world) and there is considerable rise and fall, depositing a lot of filthy mud. Because of this most canoeists finish at Monmouth, but if tide times are chosen correctly there is interesting water and scenery to Tintern or Chepstow."

"Tides. As previously stated Bristol Channel tides are the second highest in the world, with a 40ft difference between High Water and Low Water. All of this is not felt in the River Wye, but there is sufficient effect to need consideration. High Water (HW) at Tintern is four hours before Dover, or about the same as at Sharpness. The tide does not come up until an hour or so before the time of HW, but the ebb is slower. This is particularly noticeable when the moon is full or new. If going through to Chepstow, the last landing is at Tintern. It is advisable to leave here up to one hour before the tide turns. By doing this Chepstow is reached before the water has dropped much and landing is not so muddy."

"Between Tintern and Chepstow at Low Water (LW) several awkward weirs are exposed and landing on the soft mud banks is impossible. At HW the run is smooth and with no water hazards. At Chepstow below the road bridge and before the railway bridge make for a flight of steps right. If the tide has not ebbed far, landing is fairly clean, but if it has dropped much the mud over the steps will have to be waded through. There are no camping facilities here. Going further is not advised."

"Severn Estuary. The tidal part below Gloucester is not recommended because of the great range of tides and the shifting sandbanks. The upper part of the estuary is by-passed by the Gloucester and Berkeley Ship Canal which leaves the

Information about the Waters

estuary at Sharpness. Commercial craft do not use the tideway between here and Gloucester. The canal is primarily a means of getting shipping from the Bristol Channel, via the Severn estuary at Sharpness, to Gloucester, but canoeing is permitted and it makes an interesting extension of a Severn cruise. It is nearly 17 miles long and the second largest ship canal in the country. There are several picturesque swing bridges with curious porticoed houses. The canal traffic can be dense with tankers and coastal vessels approaching or leaving Gloucester. When approaching these vessels it is better to give them as wide a berth as possible. Audible warning should be given to the bridge keepers when nearing a bridge. All the bridges on this canal are swing bridges. All are painted white and have white buttresses."

"The sand and mud in the estuary makes a treacherous bottom. Landing over it is impossible in most places. The special Ordnance Survey One-Inch map of the Wye Valley and Lower Severn shows the estuary from Gloucester to the mouth of the River Wye. This gives an indication of sandbanks, which dry out at LW, but as they shift the map cannot be regarded as always accurate. Canoeing the estuary on an ebb tide could result in being caught in a dead-end channel between drying sandbanks, without an opportunity of getting out until the next tide. Because the prevailing wind is against the ebb tide (South-west wind) conditions may be choppy in exposed places. This is a great expanse of water with many potential hazards. The speed of water is usually upwards of 6 knots, so a canoeist cannot paddle against a foul tide. The Severn bore is world famous. This is a tidal wave which rushes up the Severn and the author emphasizes that he does not advise any canoeist to use the Severn Estuary. However, for the benefit of any who, nevertheless, intend to go on the waters he offers the following suggestions: Sharpness, from the canal to the mouth of the Wye, is 13 miles. This is simplest if done on a rising tide, leaving Beachley, near the mouth of the Wye and under the motorway bridge about 2 hours before HW. Care is needed to avoid wrong channels. In normal conditions this can be done and the canal entered by its sea lock to reach Gloucester."

River Severn

"From Stourport to Gloucester the river is a navigation and used by larger craft; their wash is considerable. They do not give way to canoes. There is no fee to be paid nor any need to obtain permission to use part of the Severn, but fees are charged at the few locks on the navigable part of the river. The six locks are large, and portaging may be tricky: it is usually advisable to go through them. In any case the fee is due to the lock keeper whether any craft is taken 'through, by or over' the locks."

"The tide makes itself felt up to a few miles below Tewkesbury. It is not a serious hazard. At its highest point it causes a rise of water without reversal of the current. Like the Wye, supplies are obtainable at sufficiently frequent intervals for much reserve food to be unnecessary and campsites are easily obtained."

Staffordshire and Worcestershire Canal

"A lock-keeper is in attendance at Stourport locks during daylight hours. The operation of the other locks will not be found difficult. Canoeists will have to work the locks themselves and must provide their own handle or windlass. A licence must be obtained before using the canal and its locks. From Stourport to Kinver there are 8 locks; expect an average of 15 minutes at each."

Information about the Waters

None of this information persuaded Dave and Jim to change their plans. But Rog was concerned about crossing the estuary safely. He insisted they did not have enough knowledge of the tide times and the correct route across from Chepstow to Sharpness. He took it upon himself to write to the Harbour Master at Sharpness. In his letter he stated he would be sailing out of the Wye from Chepstow to Sharpness sometime between April 19th and April 22nd and could the Harbour Master advise him of the times of the tides and suggest a safe route. In due course he received a reply (shown on the next page).

The letter was the final clincher. It seemed positive and in no way said "Don't do it". The route was confirmed. Equipment was gathered and transport organised to Glasbury.

Editor's note: The positives gleaned from this research reveal "Simple rapids; popular; moderate experience; no obstructions; water is clean; interesting; run is smooth; no water hazards; landing fairly clean; sufficiently experienced; interesting extension; picturesque; simplest if done on a rising tide; not a serious hazard; food and campsites easily obtained; locks not difficult; lock keeper in attendance; low neaps." This was very encouraging, but did we miss anything? Almost certainly: "wading unavoidable; considerable rise and fall; filthy mud; second highest tide in the world; need consideration; advisable to leave here; finish at Monmouth: leave Tintern one hour before the tide turns; 'interesting scenery'; awkward weirs; landing impossible; going forward not advised; not recommended; no camping facilities at Chepstow; shifting sandbanks; treacherous bottom; landing impossible; map cannot be regarded as accurate; choppy and potential hazards; 6 knots speed of water; cannot paddle against it; author advises – do not use the Severn Estuary; avoid wrong channels; wash is considerable; must provide their own handle or windlass; licence must be obtained; extremely

BRITISH WATERWAYS BOARD

Telephone: Sharpness 228

Your Ref.
Our Ref. HHB/MP

When telephoning please ask for
Captain H.H. Burbidge.

SHARPNESS DOCKS,
DOCK OFFICE,
SHARPNESS, GLOS.

Please reply to
Harbour Master.

29th March, 1967.

Mr. R. Annoble,
78. Hassock Lane (S),
Shipley,
Heanor, Derbyshire.

Dear Sir,

    Your letter of the 23rd instant written to the Section Inspector has been handed to me for reply.

    Times of High Water at Sharpness on April 19th will be 2.48 a.m. & 3.59 p.m.   April 20th, 4.40 a.m. & 5.38 p.m.   April 21st 6.08 a.m. & 6.48 p.m.   April 22nd 7.09 a.m. & 7.40 p.m. all times being British Summer Time.   These are low neaps.   Times of High Water at Beachley are about 25 minutes before Sharpness.

    It would be extremely difficult to define the route from Beachley to Sharpness in a letter, but briefly it is as follows, Beachley into Slime Road, Slime Road up to Inward Rocks on the North Shore then across the River to Shepperdine and up the South Shore passing Hills Flats buoy and Haywards Buoy. Haywards Buoy to Fishing House Leading Lights then past Berkeley Power Station where you can see the entrance to Sharpness formed by two wooden piers standing in the River. Total distance about 9 miles. At the Pier is a tall mast with a crossyard near the top. If there is a black ball at the end of the yard you must stay outside until the ball is dropped.

    Charts may be obtained at W.F. Price, Marine Optician, 28. Gloucester Road, Avonmouth.

Yours faithfully,

H.H. Burbidge
Harbour Master.

Merchandise is carried and stored subject to the British Waterways Board terms and conditions of carriage and storage, copies of which can be obtained on application.

Roger wrote on the back of this letter:
"High Water at Beachley:
April 19: 3.34pm
April 20: 5.13pm
April 21: 6.23pm
April 22: 7.15pm."

difficult to define the route from Beachley to Sharpness in a letter." Hmm. More negatives than positives? We were young; we weren't going to let such things stand in our way. But on reflection, did we understand the timing of the tides? We did not. Did the Harbour Master at Sharpness really understand what Rog meant by "sailing out from Chepstow"? (Roger did not specify in his letter that he and his friends would be crossing the Estuary in fragile canvas canoes.) Were we about to venture into conditions that could put us at risk? We were three would-be P.E. teachers. We had a guidebook. What could possibly go wrong?

Equipment and Provisions

Canoes

Dave had the PBK 20 double canoe that he and Jim had used on the Severn the previous year. Rog managed to borrow a single kayak from the college; he was assured it was in good condition, but he did not test it. Indeed, no thought was given to emergency repair materials for the canoes' canvas outers or plywood frames. Neither canoe carried spare paddles, or had any spray covers or buoyancy aids. Basic life-jackets were acquired from the college stores.

Tents

Dave and Jim had used a two-man Vango tent on their trip down the Severn. They'd borrowed it from college and were able to do so again. Rog was also able to get a duplicate from the college equipment store. (A one-man tent was not available to him, but the larger tent was a bonus as the extra space would provide dry storage overnight for the team's equipment and supplies.) The tents were heavy, but sturdy and waterproof with groundsheets and flysheets meaning that relative comfort would be ensured each evening.

Cooking

Paraffin-fuelled Primus stoves, with two sets of Billy Cans, would enable the cooking of breakfasts and evening meals, and for boiling water for drinks of tea or coffee. Jim was concerned by the presence of paraffin aboard the canoes, often quoting the 'paraffin everywhere' episode recorded by Jerome K Jerome in *Three Men in a Boat*. To avoid a similar disaster, screw-top plastic containers were used to contain the paraffin. (Drinking water was also carried in screw-top plastic containers.) Mugs, knives, forks and spoons were packed in rucksacks. Washing-up liquid and paper towels would do for the cleaning of cooking utensils.

Food

All food carried in the canoes would be in packets or tins or sealed in wrappers. Milk would be in cartons. There would be opportunities each day to purchase food for meals, so limited rations would be taken for the first couple of days. The initial 'pantry' would consist of tinned stew, plus packets of Vesta curry. These newly available and inexpensive products had quickly become popular with college students. Their contents (beef or chicken flavour) were emptied into the cooking pots and covered with water and then brought to the boil. The dry mixture and rice soon transformed into a tasty meal. Bacon, sausage, eggs, and a loaf of bread completed the initial essentials. Biscuits (McVities of course), cheese, crisps and chocolate would be packed for lunchtime nibbles.

Clothing

This would be kept to the minimum, just enough for warmth, comfort and decency. There would not be enough storage in the canoes for bundles of extraneous clothing. Jim sourced a copy of *The Book of Canoeing* by Alec R Ellis from the college library. (This was the 1957 fourth edition of the book first published in 1935.) It contained the following advice: "A word on the most suitable dress for canoeing is perhaps not out of place here. The idea is to wear as little as possible, both from the health point of view, and to avoid discomfort in the event of getting wet, and also because of the necessity, occasionally of wading or putting the feet in water to refloat the craft if it is grounded. A bathing slip and shorts or a bathing costume is all that is required in warm weather and gives much-appreciated freedom for paddling. Shorts and rubber soles, without stockings, is the proper dress for the lower part of the body. Incidentally, if an accident should occur and the canoe should capsize, the less clothing that is being worn the better." It all seemed sensible. But this was followed with advice on one's clothes for sleeping: "I most strongly condemn the practice, too often to be seen, of sleeping in day clothes. It is a dirty habit, most unhygienic and slovenly; take your ordinary sleeping things." "Well, stuff that!" said Roger. Pyjamas would be left at home.

Headgear

Required for warmth, and protection from the sun's rays, hats would be chosen that were practical and stylish. Rog favoured an officer's hat from the Royal Army Medical Corps that he'd been given by a relative (along with a shirt and shower-proof jacket that he would also take on the voyage). Its insignia read "In Arduis Fidelis" translated as "Faithful in Adversity". How unknowingly appropriate it would prove to be. Dave was very fond of a knitted Irish 'chunky hat' his parents had given him after their recent holiday in Ireland. He would adorn it with a swan's feather when on the river. Jim's choice of hat was unique. He was a big fan of Benny Hill, and so managed to acquire a black hat from the comedian's wardrobe. At least that's what he told everyone. The truth was equally bizarre. Originally the hat belonged to Rog's girlfriend Linda who had worn it for a few years as part of her London grammar school uniform. Rog had the hat as a spare and kindly loaned it to Jim. Did Jim make a wise choice in wearing that hat? As Benny Hill said, "Just because nobody complains doesn't mean all parachutes are perfect". All three hats, however, would provide unique styling and become an essential part of the adventurers' image. *(Fifty years later, people comment as much about the hats as the adventure. – Ed.)*

Other items

Sleeping bags were basic and protected by plastic wrappings to keep them waterproof each day when packed into the canoes. Indeed all essential items – clothing, food and equipment – would be covered in plastic sheeting to keep them dry. Priority was to ensure that cameras were encased in plastic bags when not in use. Maps and guides, with handwritten notes on possible campsites, and notebooks for the daily log, were also protected. Roger's research had revealed that locks, bridges, approaching vessels and other potential hazards should be forewarned by an audible warning signal. His solution was to take along his relative's army bugle. Musical notes he couldn't do, but 'loud' he most certainly could.

All Go, 'Come What May'

Mr Hudson, Dave's dad, agreed to transport all canoes, equipment and the three adventurers to Glasbury. He collected Rog's canoe and equipment from college the day before, while Rog and Jim travelled in Jim's car to Dave's home in Kinver. They stayed together overnight, getting ready for an early start. As they ran through their plans and checklists, they realised that no concern had been given to potential weather conditions. It was mid-April, warm and occasionally sunny, but there was just as much chance of heavy showers or night-time frosts. It was too late to seek a long-range weather forecast. They'd be on their own for twelve days, facing whatever elements or waters the voyage threw at them. It bothered them not. They were ready to depart, knowing the adventure was 'all go, come what may'.

What follows is their adventure, told in their words and with illustrations and photographs from the original log.

Ready for the off: the two canoes awaiting their adventure.

The Adventure

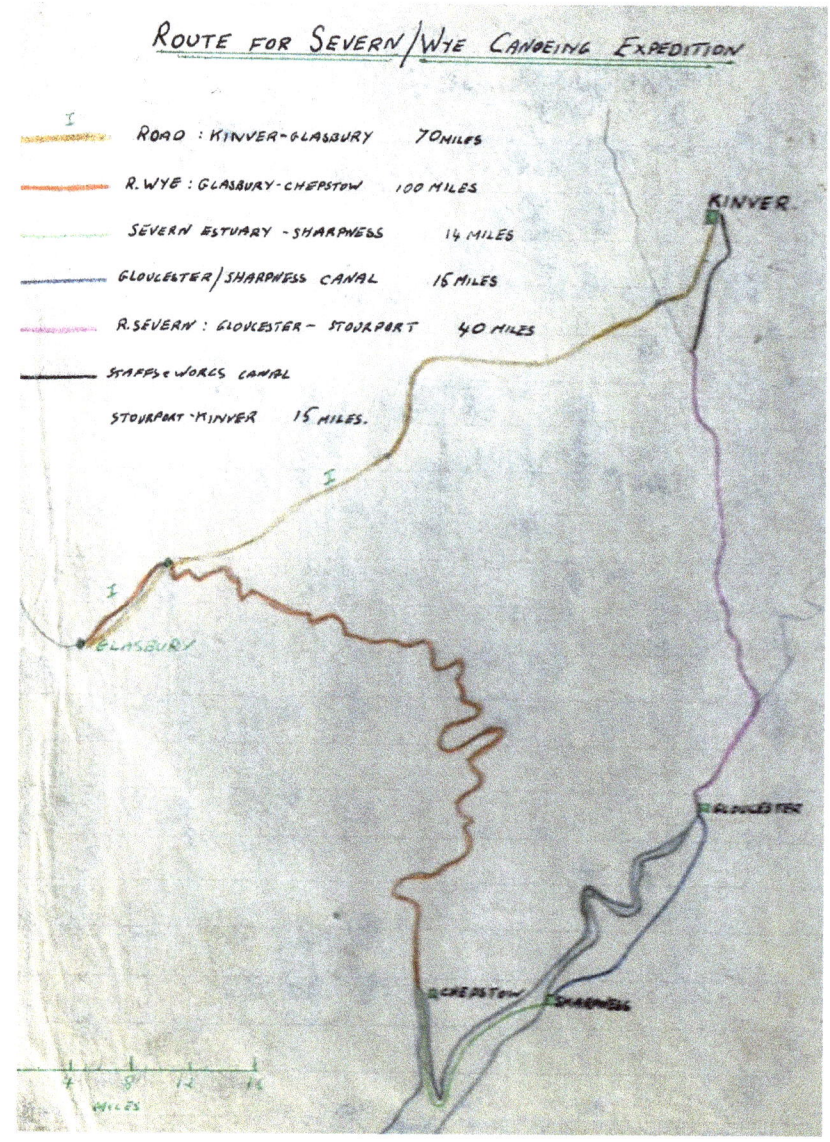

The planned route: 180 miles along two rivers, one estuary and a ship canal.

Day One
Travel to Glasbury, Making Camp

Date: Saturday 15th April 1967
Recorded by: R Annable
Weather: Warm but overcast, wind increasing in the evening.
River: Shallow, calm

"If you have never navigated the Wye, you have seen nothing."
William Gilpin, 1782

We were up early and spent quite some time loading the equipment, securing the canoes to the roof-rack of Mr Hudson's car, and generally checking that nothing had been forgotten. This was finally completed and we set out from Kinver (near Stourbridge, Worcestershire) at 11.15am. After a pleasant ride via Bewdley and Leominster we began to catch glimpses of the River Wye as it twisted and turned beside the road. Our arrival at Glasbury-on-Wye, the starting point for our adventure, was recorded at 1.15pm. Light refreshment and a ploughman's lunch was taken in the relaxed atmosphere of the Harp Inn, a typical fisherman's retreat. We asked the landlord where we could camp for the night and launch our canoes. He advised us to go across the road to the café by the bridge and enquire there. Without much difficulty we gained permission to set up camp in a field that was owned by the café proprietor, across the bridge on the opposite side of the river.

The campsite was located a quarter of a mile upstream from Glasbury bridge and could boast running water, in the form of a tap about one foot above ground level in a cowshed – that might just as well have been a cess-pool. The most frustrating part about the campsite was that although only yards from the river, the launching of canoes from this point was strictly prohibited as the banks were part of the fishing rights. The charge for the campsite was 1/6d per head; but since the café owner permitted us to use his garden and garage for storage of canoes and other equipment this was not too unreasonable. An alternative campsite, we knew, could be found near the Harp Inn but we had previously agreed to find and assess as many campsites as possible during the expedition.

Glasbury Bridge

The equipment was unloaded from the car into the field, the canoes being left in the garden of the café. We expressed our thanks to Mr Hudson for transport to Glasbury and he left to return home. Threading our way through grazing sheep, we chose a suitable spot bordered on two sides by hedges. We proceeded to set up camp.

Travel to Glasbury, Making Camp

Setting up the Glasbury camp

With the tents erected and gear suitably stowed away, we changed into shorts and sat in the sun, drinking coffee, by the side of the river. The water looked very appealing with its occasional ripples sparkling in the sunlight. Small fish were rising to take tiny flies from the surface. All very pleasant but I was anxious to get into my canoe for a practice run. By a unanimous decision we walked back to our stored canoes in the café garden and carried them to the river. Dave and Jim were confidently getting into their canoe when a slight wobble nearly capsized them. They laughed it off by claiming they had done it deliberately. I knew differently but it unsettled me. I managed to seat myself in my canoe and took my first tentative strokes with my double paddle. Amazingly I stayed upright and, very relieved, I paddled away from the bank. Dave and Jim made sarcastic hoots and cheers. I responded by shouting, "This is easy, I told you I could do it!" If only they knew how I had spent sleepless nights worrying that I would make a fool of myself.

On the river we paddled up and down easily and pleasantly, but cautiously given the shallow depth of water and fragile canvas 'skin' of the canoes. Even in mid-stream the pebbly river bottom was clearly visible. After some time it was decided to get out and inspect the first rapid. This water appeared to be a fairly easy passage except for a large wave in the middle; probably caused by a large boulder ominously near the surface. We were not sure our canoes could pass over the top safely. But it was agreed that the double canoe would attempt the passage first while I would return to fetch the cine camera and film the shooting of the rapid from the riverbank. In attempting to get out of my canoe I experienced a minor capsize, fortunately in shallow water, so I made the walk up the bank soaking wet. This incident was received with hoots of laughter from Dave and Jim and also from an elderly couple who were walking by. "Young man, you've made our day!" they said as they walked happily away.

The double canoe passed through the rapid easily, which was most disappointing considering what it looked like from the bank. However, in attempting to canoe back up the rapid Dave and Jim found the paddling against the current difficult going and were driven back down the river again; this time backwards! Now it was my turn to have a laugh at their expense. We considered that this was a suitable note to end a useful and pleasant practice session. We lined the double canoe up the rapid and then took both canoes out of the water. My single seat college canoe, I found, was awash with more water than could possibly have been caused by my minor capsize. It must have been letting in water from the moment I put it into the river. Considering the amount of water which was tipped out, it definitely needed urgent attention. This task was completed in the café garden after the café owner kindly gave me some black Bostik to seal the canvas seams. We left the canoes in the garage of the café and returned to camp hoping that the repairs would keep out the water in the future.

Outside our tents, we began preparing a meal of beef curry and boiled rice. Cooking was made difficult by the cold wind which had intensified since our return from the river. The Primus stoves were extinguished several times by the wind. We realised that shields for the flames were essential if we were to cook anything. We found some logs by the hedge and they proved excellent improvised shields when placed around the stoves. The meal was quickly prepared and enjoyed. We'd learned from our cooking experience, knowing that in more extreme conditions we would have to cook inside the tents. Jim was concerned we might not be able to cook our breakfast if the stoves kept going out.

The evening was spent in the village chatting to two locals in the Harp Inn. They told us of the inexperienced canoeists who used the river and the dangers and problems they created. I did not enlighten them that I had not been in a canoe until today. We returned to camp at 11.00pm and turned in for an early night, hoping for an early start in the morning.

Setting up and packing away the tents would become second nature

Travel to Glasbury, Making Camp

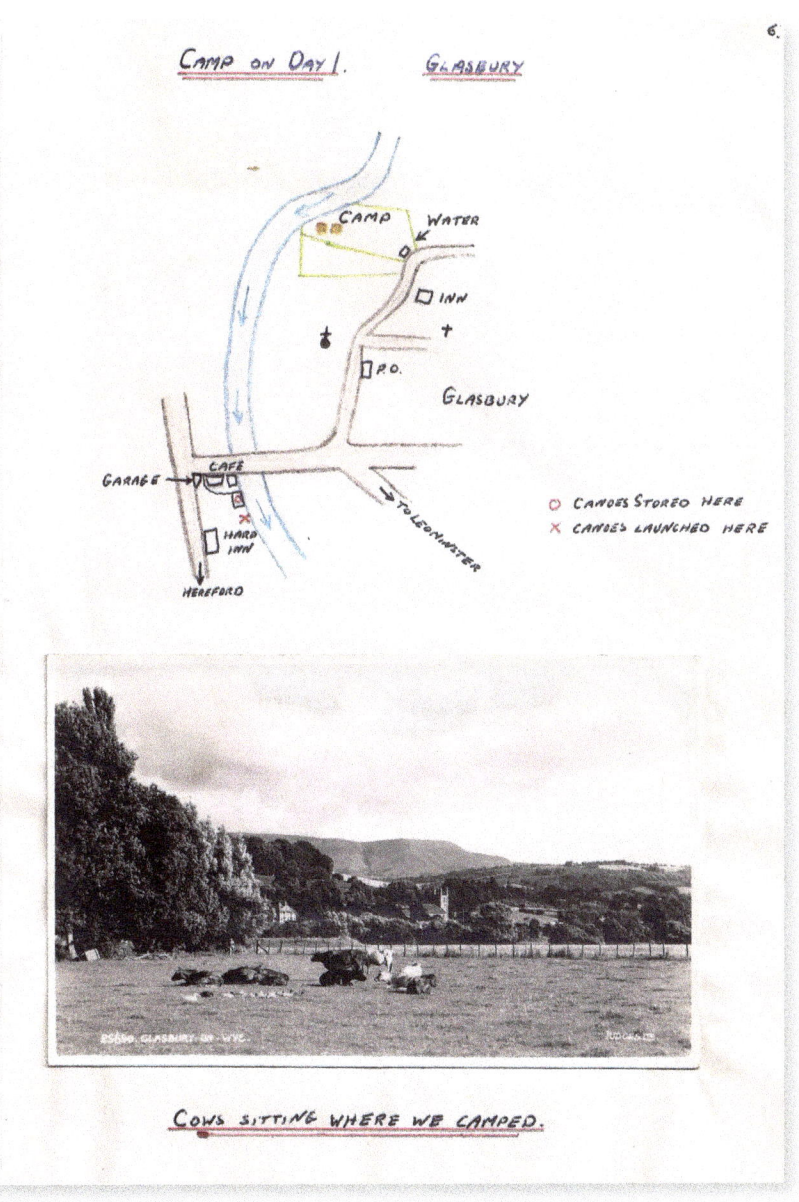

Cows sitting where we camped.

DAY 2.

GLASBURY - BREDWARDINE.

- Glasbury — first campsite
- small rapids (obstructions).
- Llowes
- 4½
- Hay on Wye
- Wyecliffe Weir
- rocky reefs below bridge.
- 8 — Shallow rapid
- Clifford — Clifford Castle
- 10 — spikes round base of bridge.
- Whitney
- rapid
- 16
- several small rapids
- Bredwardine — 19½ — rapids campsite.

N

Key (for all maps).
- major roads
- minor roads
- villages/towns

Day Two
Glasbury to Bredwardine

Date: 16th April 1967
Recorded by: R 'Jim' Murton
Weather: dry/sunny
River: shallow, clear, winding
Distance travelled: 19.5 miles

I woke early to the sound of a cuckoo calling his familiar refrain of "Cuckoo, Cuckoo". Today was the 16th of April and I couldn't recall hearing this bird so early in the year. Back home in Leicestershire we expect the cuckoo to arrive about St. George's Day, April 23rd. Perhaps this was an omen for a good beginning to our travels? The bright sunny morning encouraged us to get going. Breakfast of bacon and egg, then washing up, dismantling the tents and packing everything carefully away.

We hoped to make it to our canoes at the river in one lift and get paddling by 10.00am. However, we were delayed by the amount of gear we had to carry. If our camp had been by the riverbank we could have been away earlier, but we had to carry our equipment nearly half a mile to the river from our campsite. We laid out all our belongings by the canoes and wondered how we were going to pack them all in. This was neglect on our part; we had not tried packing the canoes before leaving home. Our departure was delayed further due to us having to repair Rog's canoe – again. We found it was leaking badly even before we started. We made another repair, repacked the canoe and, crossing our fingers, put it in the water. All appeared satisfactory. The sealant seemed to be doing a good job and no leaks emerged. At twelve noon we finally left the bridge at Glasbury. We were hoping to reach our planned next camp, nearly 20 miles downstream at Bredwardine, by tea-time. At first we made slow progress. Rog was still getting used to his canoe and discovering the correct technique for paddling in a straight line.

Roger sets off from Glasbury

The first main obstacle we came to was Wyecliff Weir. Well, the obstacle wasn't so much the weir itself but the man who was fishing beneath it. We beached the canoes above the weir to find the safe passage down. We asked the fisherman if it was alright for us to come through. He was very friendly but proceeded to tell us how he and his three friends had paid £65.00 each for the day's fishing on that particular stretch of water. He also told us the fishing would be no good for at least an hour-and-a-half if we canoed through. Not wishing to upset him we lined our canoes down the weir, with very little disturbance, walked the canoes 30 yards further downstream and set off again. As we paddled on we realised how true the old proverb is that 'it is easy to part a fool from his money'.

We moved on down towards Hay Bridge and noticed how low the water was. Dave and I were more worried than Rog about running aground and possibly damaging our canoe as our draught was much deeper. On reaching Hay Bridge we sent Rog ahead to find the best passage for our old barge. He got through alright and waved us on. We followed, only to run aground just beyond the bridge. We had to get out and refloat the canoe a few yards downstream. This was to our embarrassment but much to the delight and ribald comments of the people who were standing watching us from the bridge. Dave and I were pleased we could bring a little happiness into their lives. Rog was very helpful to us in our predicament. He just sat back and laughed. We took it at a comfortable pace moving down towards Clifford Castle. The weather was perfect during the afternoon and once we rested for a cigarette and admired the scenery. (We also had a pee break, something that we realised needed scheduling into our itinerary.)

On reaching Clifford Castle there was a small island in the centre of the river. This was not mentioned in Blandford's itinerary. We paused for a few minutes, trying to decide which side of the island we should pass. Rog decided it should be the right, Dave and I thought the left. We went our separate ways. We waited below the island for Rog to appear. He didn't. But then we saw him. About a third of the way round the island he had run aground and the current had forced him sideways. It was our turn to sit back and laugh as we watched him struggling to get out of the canoe and lift it off the rocks. (We chose not to tell Rog that we also had run aground, just the once, going to the left. As Rog hadn't seen us, we told him that our passage to the

Three Men in Two Canoes

Clifford Castle

Whitney toll bridge

Glasbury to Bredwardine

left was easy. We were, after all, the 'more experienced' canoeists.)

We paused at Whitney Toll Bridge to take photographs of this iconic structure, still apparently collecting payment from motorists travelling to and from Hay-on-Wye.

As the day wore on it became clear we were getting tired, and our progress slowed. Dave and I should have expected this as we had not done any canoeing since last year. Rog was putting on a brave face but it was obvious the mental and physical strain of his first canoeing day was draining him. We all mentioned that at no time did we feel out of breath; just suffering from what 'Blackjack' Middleton would call "local fatigue", but generally known at college as being knackered.

Eventually with light beginning to fade, Bredwardine Bridge was sighted at 8 o'clock. We were all pleased that we had successfully reached our pre-arranged 'campsite'. We passed under the bridge knowing, as explained in our Blandford itinerary, that the place to camp was on the right bank. As we beached our canoes we spotted a recently-erected sign from the Moccas estate which said that camping and even landing of canoes was prohibited on their land. "Offenders," it said, "would be prosecuted". We had a major dilemma as we could not land anywhere else. The banks were too steep and the ground above them was unsuitable for our tents. It was getting dark and we had no time to find another landing place. So, we decided to risk being prosecuted. We pulled our canoes out of the river and dragged them up the bank.

It was now nearly dark. Perhaps we could leave the canoes by the river and camp nearby? Rog and I left Dave looking after the canoes while we tried to obtain permission to camp somewhere else. The evening had cooled rapidly and we were shivering while we searched. We tried a nearby farm but the farmer's wife said that she dare not give us permission in case the landlord of the Moccas estate found out. She recommended a farm further up the road, about a quarter of a mile away from the river. We trudged uphill. The farmer of the smallholding was pleased to allow us to camp in a field behind his barn for a small fee of three shillings. We returned to the river and gave Dave the good news of our success. We soon realised that it would be another late start the following morning because, as we unpacked the canoes, we found that both canoes would need some repairing before another day's canoeing could be undertaken.

We continued to labour in the darkness to carry our equipment uphill, to the site of our distant camp, and erect our two tents. We could not transport our canoes as well. They were too heavy for us to carry that far, so we hid them the best we could under a hedge near the river, hoping no one in authority would spot them.

The farmer showed us the water tap behind his barn and also pointed out the privy we could use. We asked him why the other campsite at Bredwardine was no longer allowed. He explained that there were fishing rights difficulties and that the site had been abused by a canoeing holidays company with its unsupervised clients.

We were ready and glad to cook what we felt was a well-earned meal. It was pitch black when we began cooking, so the three of us cooked and ate by candlelight in Dave's and my tent. After the meal of beef stew, I wrote up the day's log and noted that we planned to reach Hereford tomorrow. After chatting about the day's incidents, we sought out our sleeping bags. The day had caught up with us.

We were soon asleep.

Glasbury to Bredwardine

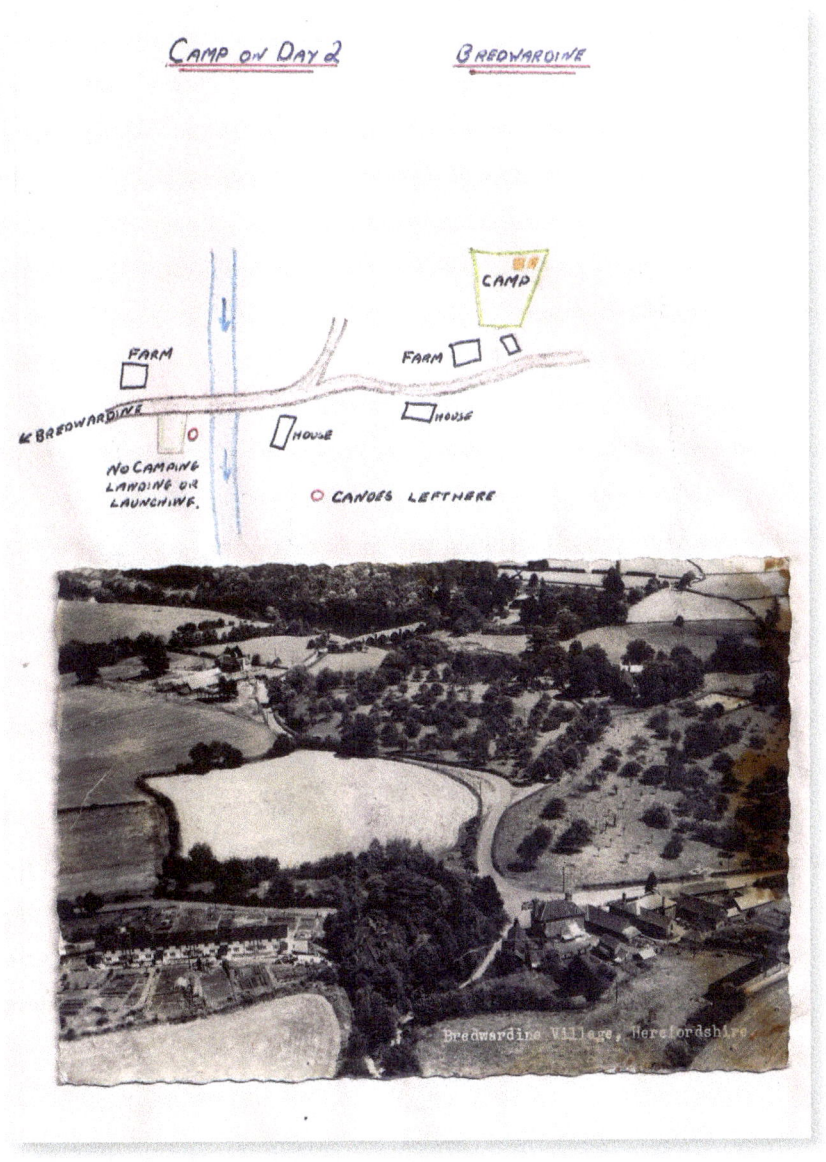

Bredwardine bridge

DAY 3.

BREDWARDINE - CAMP INN.

- Bredwardine — campsite
- the Scar (wooded cliff).
- 22 Monnington bridge (dismantled).
- Monnington
- Monnington Falls
- Byford
- 26 Bridge Sellers — Weedy shallows
- New Weir (no weir). (high walled garden).
- Lower Eaton
- 30½ — small rapid.
- Camp Inn — campsite

N

Day Three
Bredwardine to Camp Inn above Hereford

Date: 17th April 1967
Recorded by: David Hudson
Weather: warm and sunny. Evening cold
River: fast, shallow, clear
Distance travelled: 11 miles

We finished breakfast and washing-up by 9.30am. Packing was slow as everything had to be bundled so that we could make it back to the river in one lift. On reaching the river at 11.00am we examined the single canoe and saw that it needed further sealing along the canvas joints. While Jim and I made busy with the tube of Bostik, Rog hitched a lift into the village of Bredwardine to buy our food supplies. It was so warm, the Bostik remained tacky and we had to place the canoe under a hedge to take advantage of the shade to cool the hull.

Rog returned with provisions and some ice lollies. The canoes were packed and put in the water. We moved off at 1.15pm, free at last of the worry of being confronted by an irate landlord.

Progress was leisurely. We reached Monnington Falls at 3.00pm. This white-water rapid was considered the most serious water hazard for anyone canoeing from Glasbury. An island near the left bank is joined to the right bank by a rocky reef. All of the water falls over rocks into the left channel. There are overhanging trees in the channel below.

Three Men in Two Canoes

We beached safely above the rough water and walked downstream to inspect the hazard. It was decided that Jim and I would attempt the rapids first in our double canoe while Rog filmed our progress.

The rapids, with their deep waves and strong swirling currents, were the most difficult but exhilarating that Jim and I had ever encountered. Although water swirled from the bows into the cockpit we remained stable and shot down the channel, just missing a fallen tree. On rejoining the main river below the island, we beached and walked back to Rog at the top of the rapid. He was enthusiastic about the film he had taken. We then planned how best to record his progress in the single canoe. Rog said he would blow his bugle to forewarn us when he was on his way. Jim selected a vantage point above the initial rapid, as he was using the cine camera, while I waded into the fast flow to take my snapshots.

Rog quickly donned his lifejacket and manoeuvred his canoe away from the bank. As he approached the faster water he gave a confident but premature blast on his bugle. He hit the front of the wave correctly and seemed to be going well, but his glide down the main current took him further to the left than we had gone. In this fast current he had insufficient time to avoid the tree lying in midstream. He achieved what can only be described as a 'head on collision' with the partially-submerged tree. (He assures us he did it on purpose.) With the bows wedged, the stern was forced round by the current. In this wedged broadside, a capsize was inevitable. Seeing Rog's desperate plight Jim and I dashed downstream – and took some more photographs. Once we had enough film in the can we waded out and retrieved Rog and the sinking canoe from around the tree. This was no easy task, for the current was trying to force the now drenched canoe into the maze of roots.

Bredwardine to Camp Inn above Hereford

Looking for leaks

Warning sign from the Moccas estate

The Scar wooded cliff

Monnington Falls

Below the falls

Roger inspects the rapid

Roger approaches the rapid

Roger enters the rapid

Bredwardine to Camp Inn above Hereford

Roger moves down the rapid

Disaster ahead!

Roger hanging on before rescue

Peering into the swirl we could see the remains of another canvas canoe that had obviously suffered the same fate. Diving in to recue Rog, we used all our strength to lever and extricate the canoe from around the tree and move it to the bank. Here we tipped out sufficient water to enable Rog to re-float the canoe and move downstream to calmer water.

Jim and I walked back to our canoe and crossed the river to where Rog was waiting, dripping wet and glad to be alive. It was a relief to find the canoe was undamaged but everything in it, regardless of waterproof covering, was soaked. This included all Rog's clothes and our food. Fortunately, we had packed Rog's sleeping bag in our canoe and the bulk of the food was tinned. Taking advantage of our spare clothing, Rog made a quick change into dry attire. At this point we could have enjoyed a cigarette but all forty of them had failed the water test in the single canoe. On checking the contents of his canoe, Rog found he had lost his blue shorts and his bugle.

Unperturbed, we sallied forth again. By 6.00pm the weather had turned cold and we decided to camp at the nearest convenient site. We were not too sure of the camping in this area, for we had hoped to reach Hereford today. However, a sign advertising the "Camp Inn" reminded me that a school had camped here the previous summer. We landed and hauled the canoes up the bank but not without Rog adding further to his problems by finding the only cowpat in the area to step in. Leaving the canoes, we followed the footpath up a cliff to the Camp Inn where we enjoyed a good beer and a warming open fire. The landlord gave us permission to camp in the field where we had landed: this was a stroke of good luck because apparently this was the only land in the area (owing to the fishing rights) where camping was allowed. Having purchased some crisps, to replace our ruined bread, we returned

Bredwardine to Camp Inn above Hereford

to the river and set up camp.

While we prepared a curry, Rog decorated the surrounding trees with his 'washing' in the hope his clothes would dry out overnight. After an excellent meal we retired to the inn where we spent a pleasant evening. (It is true that for the first time in two days Jim was able to appreciate the luxury of relieving himself in modern conveniences.)

We prepared for bed at 11.30pm. We hoped to get an early start in the morning.

I TOLD ROG TO KEEP THE RICE IN A PLASTIC BAG!

Upstream from the cliff at The Camp Inn

Downstream from The Camp Inn

Bredwardine to Camp Inn above Hereford

16th Century Wye Bridge, Hereford.

DAY 4.

CAMP INN – FOWNHOPE.

- Camp Inn — Campsite
- small rapid
- deep water to Hereford
- 35 Hereford
- small rapid
- dangerous currents
- 39 Hampton Bishop
- River Lugg
- 42 Mordiford
- 45 Fownhope — Campsite

N

Day Four
Camp Inn to Fownhope

Date: 18th April 1967
Recorded by: Roger Annable
Weather: sunny, warm with cool breeze
River: shallow with good current
Distance travelled: 14.5 miles

There was no dawn chorus this morning. The cuckoo must have overslept. We did not stir until 9.00am. Windy weather made cooking difficult and our breakfast of bacon and egg was some time being prepared. Jim insisted on opening a tin of baked beans. I joked that perhaps they would provide us with a downstream wind. It was alright for me on my own in the single canoe but Dave would have the full blast of Jim in front of him in the double. Afterwards we broke camp, not wind, and everything was ready to be loaded into the canoes except for an array of my clothes fluttering in the breeze; rapidly recovering from the soaking of yesterday. Waiting for them to dry, we began filming the beautiful views of the river upstream and down. Once my clothes were dry, we were able to load the canoes.

Eventually we left Caton Camp at 12.40pm and we were on our way to Hereford.

For a few miles the river meandered, creating a number of interesting easy rapids. Gradually the rapids became less and less frequent and long straight stretches appeared. The wind began to blow stronger, creating a nice exciting swell underneath the

Three Men in Two Canoes

Leaving Caton Camp

Hereford Ahoy!

canoe to break the monotony of straight stretches. With the bows dipping into the swell and washing over the decks we sped on at a good pace.

As we approached Hereford, a delicious aroma of cider filled the air. Upon investigation we discovered that it was coming from a cider factory beside the river.

The sun was shining brightly as we pulled under the new road bridge at Hereford and secured our craft to iron spikes and lumps of concrete.

We complimented ourselves on making such good time (we had covered 5 miles in about 50 minutes). We made our way into the city to collect supplies. Once in the main street we decided that a meal was called for and thus we entered a restaurant; where we were greeted by concerned and visibly disturbed waitresses. One was heard to murmur "Good grief, look at this lot!" Certainly, our dishevelled appearance was not in keeping with the rest of their customers or the local community. They did, however, take our order and serve us. We ate a hearty meal of fish and chips, then left – probably to the relief of the restaurant's staff and customers.

I was very concerned that since I had lost my bugle, I needed a replacement. I still felt I wanted to be able to warn other craft and lockkeepers of our approach. I went into a cycle shop and found just the thing: a bicycle horn bugle with squeezable rubber bulb. It made a very loud retort when I squeezed it; just the job. This shop also sold us paraffin for our Primus stoves. We collected our food supplies from a supermarket, which made for quick easy shopping.

We agreed that a number of historical places merited careful filming and undertook to complete this task. The most notable were the 'Old House' of 1621 vintage and the beautiful cathedral. During filming an elderly gentleman became inquisitive and after a short chat he went on his way confidently believing he would soon achieve fame by appearing with Jonathan Routh on his famous Candid Camera television programme. This, and the way we had been received by the people of Hereford, amused us greatly. We had met with a mixed reception – the men viewing us with amusement and the ladies with extreme caution.

We continued on our way at 3.30pm in pleasantly warm weather. Two miles downstream of Hereford we were delayed by fishermen who were fishing through a rapid in the main channel of the river. We took this opportunity to film an unusual modern house and provide the fishermen with information about catches of fish along the river. The run to Fownhope was pleasant and steady with several pauses to admire the beautiful scenery and soak up the sunshine. At the 42-mile mark from our start at Glasbury, where the River Lugg enters the Wye from the left, we saw the first reasonable-sized salmon being caught. Canoeing at this point seemed much easier. We had all adjusted ourselves to the conditions and I was confident I had settled into a steady rhythm. We arrived at Fownhope at around 7.00pm and located the field which we knew had been used by a previous Saltley College party in 1961. Two fishermen were crossing the river in a punt at this point. We decided to await their arrival and enquire where permission to camp in this spot could be obtained. We assisted these two elderly anglers to get out of their punt, holding it firmly while they climbed onto land – much to their appreciation – and they gave us the directions to the landowner. After a pleasant walk through the fields we arrived at the appropriate farm where we gained permission to camp on payment of a shilling a head. We were thankful to have a site on the riverbank with the canoes on dry land beside us. Together we unloaded the canoes making use of the fishermen's punt to transfer equipment from our canoes into it and then

Hereford Cathedral

The 'Old House' Hereford

Modern house below Hereford

to the bank. (The banks were quite high and loaded canoes could not be taken straight out of the water.) With all the equipment in the fishermen's punt, Dave and Jim joked that there was more room there than in our two canoes combined and that we should continue our journey in this craft. However, Jim's ability to unpick the padlock, which secured the craft to the bank, was pathetic and the idea was abandoned.

Setting up camp was completed as per usual with Dave and Jim pitching the tents, and me cooking the meal and stowing away the gear. Having eaten, we set out for the Highland Home Inn which our Saltley predecessors had recommended in their log. Upon arrival at the directed location we found the inn was no longer the "Highland Home" but rather the "Flamenco". There was no indication of a public bar so we were obliged to enter the lounge which was expensively furnished in a Spanish or South American theme. Although we felt rather embarrassed in the 'selective' atmosphere and the plush surroundings, we were eventually able to relax. Albeit to the tunes of the smooth flamenco music playing in the background, the dim lights and our rather expensive drinks.

There was some debate as to which nationality was being portrayed in this room and Dave insisted that it was Spain. From this he deduced that a door displaying the sign "Senoras" was for his use. He obviously had confused his Senors (sirs) with his Senoras (ladies). Ignoring a smaller sign showing a handbag and gloves, he strode boldly across the room. Much to the horror of the ladies in the room, who could not stop him before he reached the door, Dave pushed his way in. The mistake was realised – but we also were too late to stop him. Needless to say, we beat an uncomfortably hasty retreat from the hostelry when he returned. Dave reported that the toilet was the poshest and sweetest smelling loo he had ever had the privilege to visit, but he was surprised by the lack of urinals. However, the sit-down facility was what he urgently needed. On our way out, much to our amusement and Dave's embarrassment, we noticed a similar toilet door on the other side of the room marked "Caballeros" (gentlemen). The landlord gave us a look that implied he was pleased to see us leaving. I doubt we would be welcome back anytime soon. On the walk back to our tents we chuckled over our experience in the "Flamenco". At least they hadn't stuck little pink parasols in our pints.

Back at camp, Jim made us a brew of tea and opened a packet of McVities digestive biscuits (brilliant for dunking) that he bought in Hereford earlier. It was a perfect end to a good day.

We turned in around midnight.

The old bridge at Hereford

Camp Inn to Fownhope

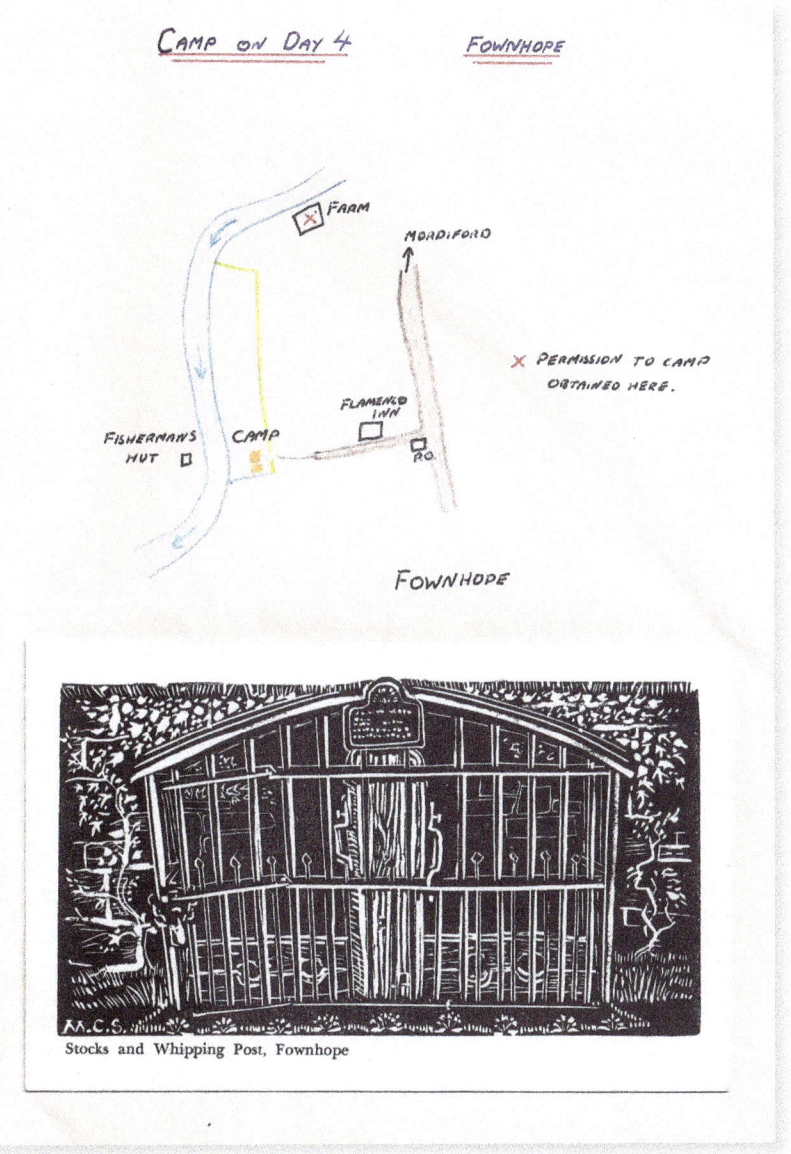

Stocks and Whipping Post, Fownhope

DAY 5.
FOWNHOPE - ROSS on WYE

- 45 Fownhope camp site — small rapid
- Wellingham
- 47
- Carey — shallows
- 51½
- Hoarwithy
- Hole in the Wall (cottages)
- 59 — rapid
- Fay
- weedy shallows
- rocky breakwater
- Bridstow
- 63
- Ross on Wye.

N

Day Five
Fownhope to Ross-on-Wye

Date: 19th April 1967
Recorded by: R 'Jim' Murton
Weather: cool, overcast, becoming very windy
River: deeper, slower and noticeably muddy
Distance travelled: 18 miles

Everything pointed to an early start from Fownhope – the campsite was right on the riverbank, we did not have to repair either of the canoes and we knew that we would have to reach the general stores at Hoarwithy Bridge before 1.00pm; Wednesday being half-day closing. We badly needed to restock our provisions. Unfortunately, we did not break camp with any sense of urgency. Therefore, we did not leave Fownhope until 11.45am with Hoarwithy six and a half miles away. Before we set off, two canoeists went by. We guessed they were father and son.

We made good time to Hoarwithy without incident. The water was very calm and canoeing was comparatively effortless. We passed the two canoeists we had seen earlier, resting on the right bank. Even though we had made good progress, we did not arrive at Hoarwithy until after one o'clock. The only shop in the village was closed. This was a big problem as there were no more villages where we could buy provisions until we reached the town of Ross-on-Wye, 11 miles downriver, and we did not expect to reach there until early evening when there would not have been any shops open, half day closing or not.

While we considered what to do, we went to the local pub, the New Harp Inn, and had a lunchtime sandwich and a pint. This was a much-enjoyed break. The landlord suggested we should go back to the shop, as the shop owner was probably still at home and would be pleased to serve us. We took his advice and went to see if the shopkeeper was still in the shop and beg for her mercy. Wandering back to the shop we again met the other two canoeists; they had also hoped to buy provisions. (We later discovered they were canoeing from Glasbury to Monmouth and realised we would be seeing more of them before we reached their destination.)

We all agreed to go to the shop; and hoped we could get served. We found the shopkeeper, at her home next-door to the shop, and she agreed to open up and serve us. Afterwards, the five of us were chatting about the lady's kindness but realised she would have been foolish not to serve us as our two orders must have been equivalent to her normal day's trade.

Our two groups set off separately. We were last away because we stopped for our customary cigarette. Very soon the calm conditions that we had experienced paddling to Hoarwithy, changed rapidly. As we pressed on to Ross-on-Wye, a high wind suddenly sprang up – making paddling against the headwind very difficult. The most noticeable and difficult stretch was the last two miles into Ross. This part of the river was straight and wide, with the wind blowing up the river. Large waves were whipped up and came pelting towards us. These were the roughest conditions we had experienced for canoeing. The wind did not affect the canoes so much as the paddles; several times the double canoe was nearly turned around by the strong wind twisting the paddles out of our control.

Fortunately, we reached Ross safely and still dry. But we

Fownhope to Ross-on-Wye

Approaching Ross on Wye

had to find a campsite. We did not think it would be too difficult, as two possible sites were listed in our itinerary. The first one we passed was in the grounds of a hotel. We thought this might be too expensive and chose to try the one at the far side of the town near the ruins of the old castle. We looked at this second site and found it to be on common land, which meant we would not have to pay for camping. This was an attractive thought but the site had its disadvantages. Firstly, it was next to the main road into Ross and secondly there was no water supply or a toilet nearby. We soon returned to the first site where the father and son canoeists had already set up their camp. I went to the hotel to enquire about camping permission. The hotel proprietor gave us permission, but when she told me the cost (eight shillings) I nearly asked her which room in the hotel she was giving us. Dave and Rog were not pleased when I told them what we'd been charged. Anyway, we calmed down, unpacked and made a good curry meal.

The campsite had one big advantage – a very good pub

only twenty yards away. Naturally we had to sample its ales. After a quick drink or two we retired to our tents. However, I soon realised the curry was working through me and I needed to sample some of the excellent toilet facilities which the proprietor said were available to us. On inspection, I soon found out that not only had she charged us extortionately but she was also a liar. The toilets were disgusting. After seeing them I asked the landlady for an alternative facility. She was less than cooperative and she pointed me towards a nearby field. 'Needs must when you have to go' and I was desperate. I found the "field" to be a public park. Not deterred, I cautiously proceeded. Almost immediately after completing my ablutions I saw a torch beam being flashed around and heard footsteps rapidly approaching me. I very quickly realised that it was a policeman with a patrol dog, making his routine check of the park. I made a hasty retreat out of the park, without being apprehended, and returned to our tent by a different route.

It wasn't my night, but at least it amused Dave and Rog. I wasn't very amused. I can't think what I'd have said in court had I been caught?

Fownhope to Ross-on-Wye

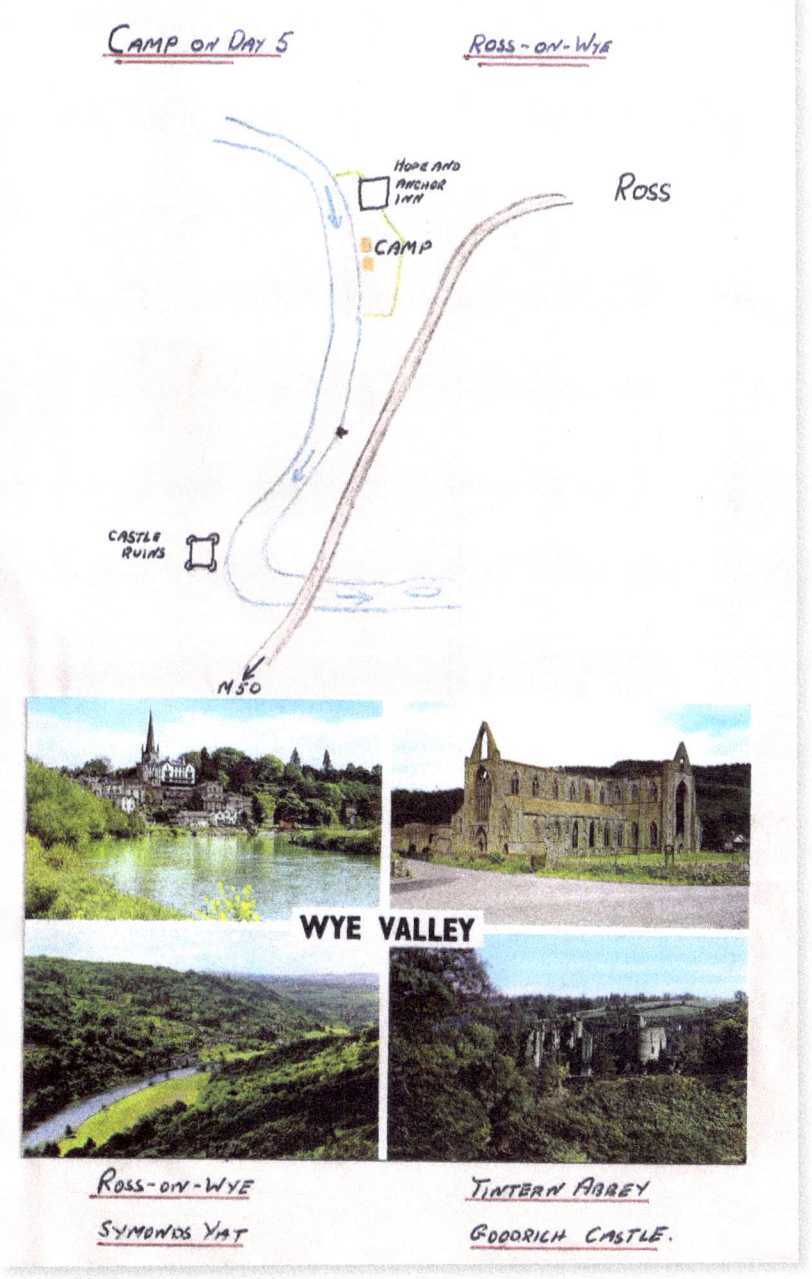

DAY 6.

ROSS on WYE — SYMONDS YAT.

- ↑ Ross on Wye
- 63 — Shallows below bridge
- Weirend
- Pencraig
- 67½ Goodrich Castle / Goodrich — Kerne Bridge — rapids below bridge
- 71 — rapid
- Symonds Yat — high rock with flagstaff, visible both sides
- Symonds Yat 77½ — long rapid — English Bicknor
- 78 Forestry Commission Camp site

N

Day Six
Ross-on-Wye to Symonds Yat

Date: 20th April 1967
Recorded by: David Hudson
Weather: wind developing, heavy rain in the evening. *River:* deep pools, straight runs except for around Yat Rock.
Distance travelled: 15 miles

We were up at 8.00am this morning. This was due to a fire siren going off in the town and waking us from our slumbers. After a breakfast of bacon, sausage and egg we went into Ross for provisions. We lost Rog when he went off to post one of his films. Thinking he was getting the shopping done, Jim and I returned to camp only to find Rog there without supplies. He thought we were going to get them. While he was sent on a further mission into town, we dismantled the tents and packed the canoes. On Rog's return we were further delayed by Rog chasing something downstream that he'd seen floating by. He'd believed the item to be the blue shorts he'd lost when he capsized at Monnington Falls. Sadly for him, his sighting turned out to be a blue Camping Gaz canister.

We left Ross at 12.40pm and made good speed to Goodrich Castle – a distance of some four and a half miles. A pleasant hour was spent sight-seeing in the castle and recording our visit on film. As we were the only visitors to the ruin, the solitude enabled us to experience the atmosphere of a bygone era. Rog was enraptured by the dungeon; Jim by a falling stone in

Approaching Goodrich Castle

Looking upriver from Goodrich Castle

Goodrich Castle

the 168 feet deep well; and me by using the ancient sanitation. We left the castle at 2.30pm, heading downstream towards Symonds Yat.

From this point downstream, we noticed a change in the scenery. The banks closed in and there were wooded slopes on both sides of the river. We had been told this area was the main tourist attraction of the Wye valley, but soon we realised that much of its unique scenery is best viewed from the river. The railway, which once crossed the area, is now defunct and its bridges are being dismantled. At Lydbrook, Rog had difficulty in negotiating the mass of ropes and cables hanging from one such bridge in the process of demolition. Jim and I had less trouble, because workmen on the bridge raised the ropes out of harm's way when we paddled through.

Shortly after Lydbrook we came in view of the towering cliffs of Symonds Yat Rock on our left. But the river continued in a large loop to come back on the other side of the Rock. Four miles round the loop and we came to Symonds Yat's commercial centre. We again met up with the father and son canoeists who were inspecting a large rapid downstream from the last dwelling. We beached and joined them. An island below directed water left into a large rapid. This rapid was deep and straight and had waves large enough to swirl up into any canoe. We watched the father and son deal competently with this hazard and then rushed back to our canoes to make our attempts. Our speed was hastened by the cold wind and the stench from a dead sheep marooned nearby. Rog, worried for his life, donned his life jacket and gave Jim his cine camera and a description of his blue shorts. Jim offered the advice "You'll be alright, you'll get over it!" It's a good job he did, for again Rog was carrying all our food. A dead cow floating down the rapid had proved an unusual obstacle for him to avoid. We followed him successfully within a few minutes; it was challenging but also exhilarating.

A mile downstream we reached our intended overnight stay at the Biblins Forestry Commission campsite. Although it was only 5.30pm the warden was nowhere to be found. Undeterred, we waited by a woodfire left burning by previous campers. Having posted the warden missing after a second search for him we set up camp and enjoyed a beef curry.

This campsite has all modern amenities and is set in a picturesque wooded valley. It caters for school and scout camps. It could provide a perfect site for any future school camp.

Looks like an early night for a change. Hope for an early start in the morning. Tintern Abbey should prove interesting and who knows, with our beards and brown smocks, we may get mistaken for monks of old and enrolled for monastic duties?

I THINK DAVE IS TAKING OUR VISIT TO TINTERN ABBEY TOO SERIOUSLY!

Symonds Yat Forestry Commisssion campsite

The suspension chain bridge at the campsite

Jim investigates the chain bridge

Three Men in Two Canoes

The view from Yat Rock

Ross-on-Wye to Symonds Yat

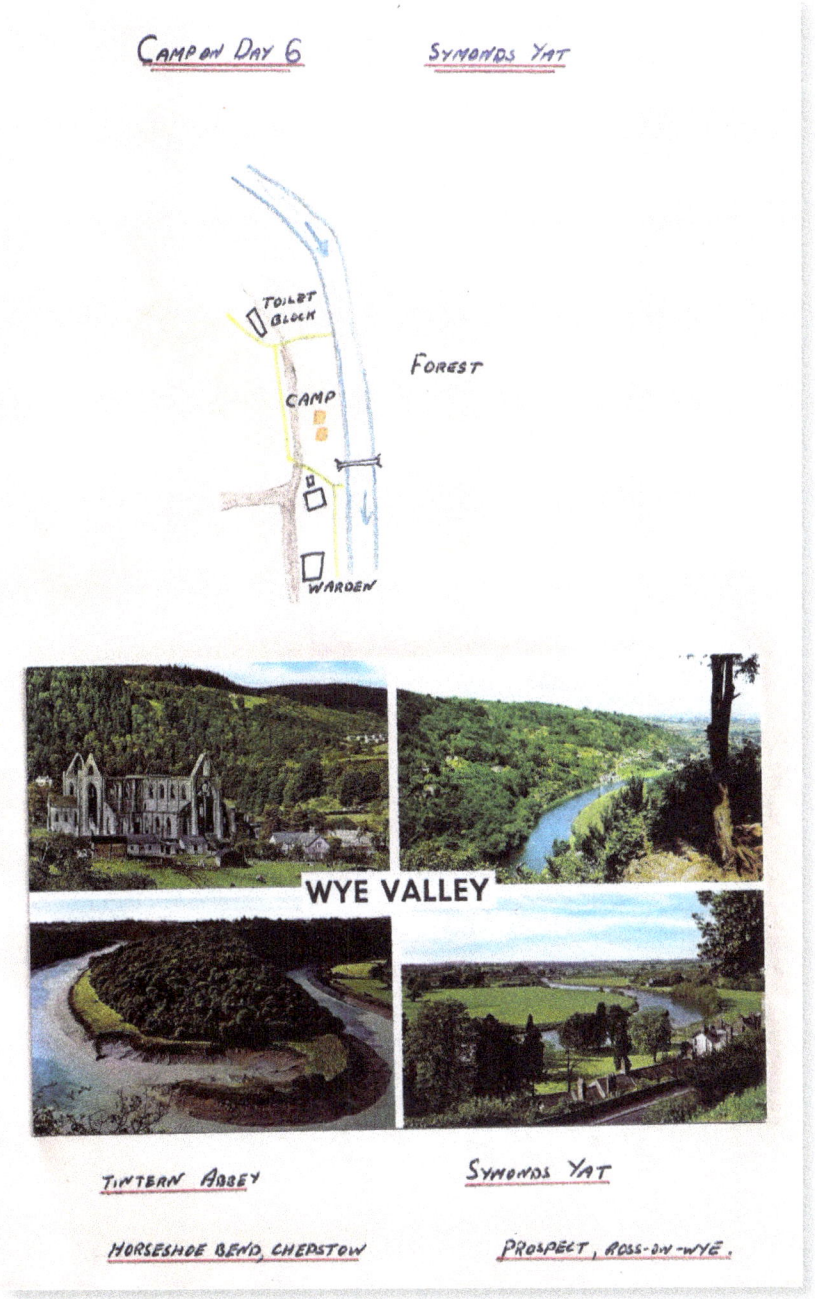

DAY 7.
SYMONDS YAT - TINTERN.

- Forrestry Commission Camp site
- 81½ Chapel Farm — Severn Sister's Rocks.
- Monmouth 84 — River Monnow
- rocky shallow rapids
- Redbrook 86½ — straight rapid
- Bigsweir Bridge
- Llandogo 91½ — rapids
- Limit of Tide
- easy rapids to Tintern
- Brockweir
- 94½ Tintern (Campsite). x Abbey

N

Day Seven
Symonds Yat to Tintern

Date: 21st April 1967
Recorded by: Roger Annable
Weather: overcast, showers at first with some wind, becoming sunny. *River:* becoming deeper and sluggish.
Distance travelled: 16 miles

We were up at 8.45am and as it was showery and windy, we cooked inside Dave and Jim's tent. We each enjoyed a very satisfying breakfast of bacon, sausage and fried egg. After we had done the washing up, Dave and Jim prepared the equipment for loading into the canoes while I walked through the forest to pay our site fees at the warden's house. Again, the warden was nowhere to be found so I returned to camp where Dave and Jim were engaged in conversation with an axe-carrying forester. This man was quite knowledgeable about the state of the river. He also filled us in with details of local history; especially connected with the railways. He talked for some time about the nearby suspension footbridge, reflecting how it swayed during the winter and made for hazardous crossing when ice formed on the steel grills. We had kept him from his work for nearly an hour – not that he was at all concerned – but then he finally resigned himself to leave us and go chop down a few more trees.

While we were breaking camp, we had to stop because of a freak cloudburst and take shelter in the one tent that was still standing. Once the deluge had finished, we were able to

Roger heading confidently to Tintern

continue packing and loading the canoes. We completed this and were ready to set off. But Dave and Jim insisted on making a final attempt to contact the warden. During their absence I filmed the river from the middle of the suspension footbridge. Once more the warden could not be found, so we launched the canoes and left at 1.15pm; silently thanking the Forestry Commission for providing us with an excellent campsite free of charge.

The father and son canoeists had still not left. They stood on the suspension bridge as we passed underneath it, wishing us good luck for the rest of our journey. We made good time over the six miles into Monmouth. We landed on the left bank by a rowing club almost immediately before Monmouth bridge at 2.20pm.

The town itself was quite an interesting one with narrow streets and small shops. We purchased our provisions and had a snack in a café called the "Crumpled Horn". The owner challenged us as to our reasons for filming his café before we entered it. We briefly explained our rivers project and he seemed impressed. Satisfied with our explanation, he left us to relax over our snack. Again, we became aware that the people we encountered were somewhat disturbed about our dishevelled appearance.

We departed from Monmouth at 4.10pm and were hit by a freak snowstorm. It didn't last long but we were soaked and cold. We had no other option but to grit our teeth and carry on. Very soon after leaving Monmouth the River Monnow entered on our right, bringing mud and debris into the Wye. Passing between a dismantled railway bridge, just below this point, we encountered two rapids close together. Our itinerary directed us to keep left at the first rapid and then swing over to take the rapid on the right. Since these directions were a little confusing, considering the actual conditions, we chose to ignore them and proceeded as best as possible. I went through the first rapid a little to the right of centre, where the main channel seemed to be, closely followed by the double canoe. All too soon I was being driven right towards the second rapid. A fisherman was wading ankle deep on the shingle bottom above this rapid. He loudly ordered me to stop. Back-paddling frantically I managed to slow down beside him. He told me the water on the right was too shallow for us to get through. He directed us to use the centre or go to the left to be safe. I waved to the double canoe, still safely behind, to go straight through on the left. Dave and Jim changed course in time and passed swiftly and safely through; I manoeuvred across to my left and followed them successfully. The fisherman was obviously not impressed and gestured theatrically.

We canoed on without further incident and reached Bigsweir Bridge – the tidal limit – one hour after leaving Monmouth. We decided not to land there as originally planned,

Three Men in Two Canoes

Monmouth Grammar School

River Wye below Monmouth Bridge

The Monnow Bridge at Monmouth

because of the condition of the banks which were steep and rising three or four feet above the river. But we paused briefly, drifting slowly downstream from the bridge. We commented on the filthy state of the river which was liberally scattered with branches, bottles, empty cardboard boxes, cans, seaweed and paper.

We pressed on towards Tintern, noticing that rapids shown on our itinerary were not visible. Obviously, they were covered by the extra water in the river brought up by the tidal surge which appeared to be steady and near its peak. Passing under Tintern Bridge and through Tintern Parva we pulled over to a small road bridge and considered how we could land. Seeing a suitable field with a small house nearby, I decided to land and enquire if we could camp there. The river was now bank-high and lapping over the grass terraced banks of the field, thus making for a difficult landing. I turned my canoe around, gained speed and made straight for the grass bank. There was a slight bump as the bow of my canoe hit the bank and slid over the wet grass. From this position it was relatively easy to swing the canoe around, step out, drag the canoe onto the grass terrace and scramble up the bank into the field. I shouted to Dave and Jim to wait while I went off to seek permission to camp in the field. This I gained from a farmer at a nearby smallholding, on the condition we behaved ourselves. Apparently camping was under threat because of the poor behaviour of others.

While I had been away, river conditions had changed tremendously. Dave and Jim were still in the water on the opposite bank patiently hanging on to a landing stage. But the tide had turned and was ebbing rapidly. Noticing the water mark on the private landing stage they calculated that the water level was dropping three to four inches every minute. My canoe was now resting on dry land several feet higher than the water, which previously had lapped against it. Dave and Jim fought their way over from the other side against the ebb tide to land their canoe near me. Together we pulled and carried the canoes up the slippery bank into the field where they could be unloaded. The camp was set up, a meal prepared and eaten. After this we retired to the "Rose and Crown" across the river and enjoyed a quiet evening. The river by now had fallen about twenty feet, exposing awkward rapids and a weir below the bridge.

No need to be up early tomorrow. We have to wait for one hour after the turn of the tide. Probably 3.00pm at the earliest before we can continue to Chepstow and cross the Severn Estuary. Hope the log will continue after a successful "E" (Estuary) Day and that we get applauded at Chepstow for our "ton up" of 100 miles. Still here in the nervous nineties.

We turned in at midnight.

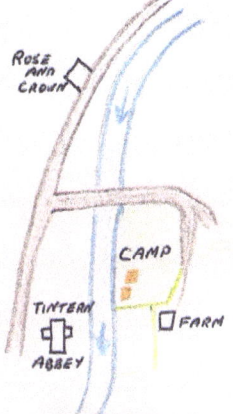

CAMP ON DAY 7   TINTERN

TINTERN ABBEY

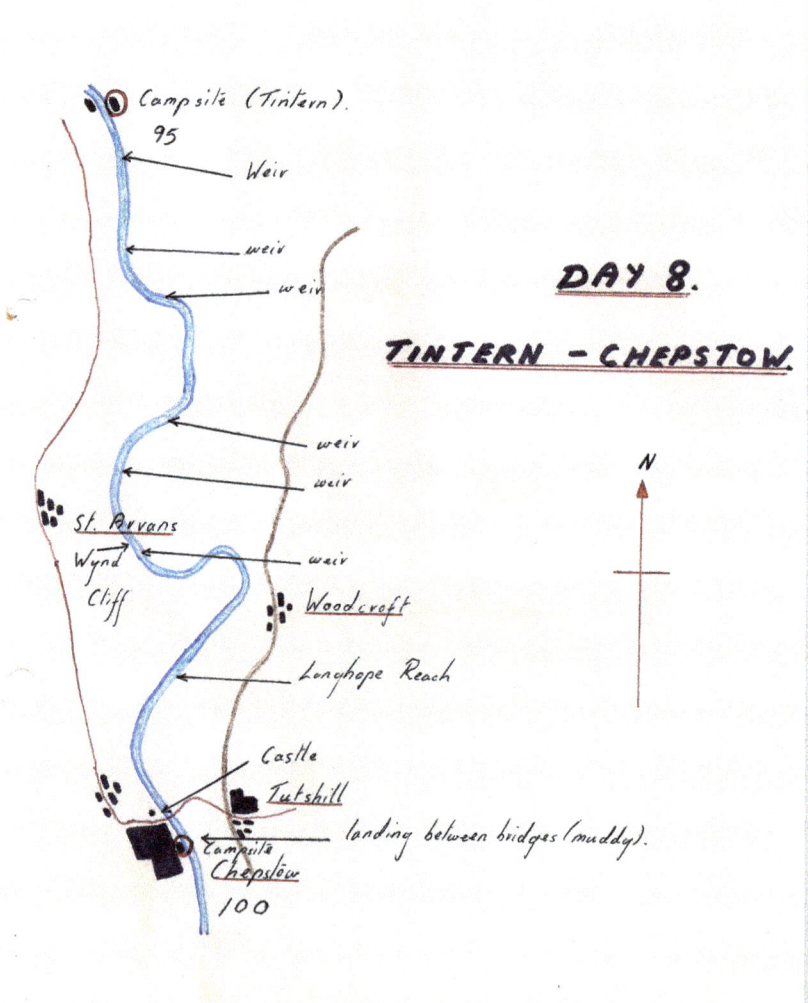

Day Eight
Tintern to Chepstow

Date: 22nd April 1967
Recorded by: R 'Jim' Murton
Weather: bright at first, becoming cold, overcast and with steady rain later
River: tidal (muddy, debris etc.)
Distance travelled: 6 miles

This was one day we did not have to get up early. The state of the predicted tide meant that we did not have to leave the campsite for the estuary crossing until 3 o'clock at the earliest. Consequently, we took our time cooking breakfast and completed the washing up at about half past ten. We took a look around our campsite and photographed a derelict waterwheel. We also found a long-abandoned vintage motor car that was rusting in the undergrowth. Somebody had painted the name "Bone" on its bonnet in graffiti. I could not resist taking my place at the steering wheel and pretending I was its driver. As I signalled a right turn I heard a click and looked up to see Dave taking a photograph of me.

We decided to see the farmer for some information about the river between Tintern and Chepstow. He sounded confident that we would have no trouble in negotiating the several weirs which lay on our route. It was essential to know this, as the time it would take us to get to Chepstow would decide whether we could make the estuary crossing in the evening. It was essential to reach Beachley, where the Wye entered the Severn Estuary,

Derelict waterwheel at the Tintern campsite

Jim in 'Bone'

by a quarter past five. Again, like others on our downriver journey, the conversation got around to the problem of canoeists finding campsites when touring. He explained how he was normally pleased to allow camping in his field, but went on to say how a holiday company (who had used his field in the past) had become a constant annoyance to him by the lack of supervision and very poor behaviour of its clients.

We could not leave Tintern without having a look around the abbey, so we chose to spend some time filming in the grounds; and later buying our day's provisions at the only store in the village. The visit to the abbey proved to be very worthwhile, but again our weather-beaten appearance aroused several comments from the many tourists who were visiting. Rog and I thought Dave looked quite acceptable; his small neat beard and long brown anorak with hood (looking very much like a monk's habit) seemed to blend in very well with the surroundings of a Monastic Age.

After buying the necessary provisions, we wandered back to the campsite to make ready for our departure. We all admitted that the estuary crossing was going to be the most exciting and dangerous part of our project. Because of this, we were looking forward to it more than anything else.

With everything packed and the canoes checked over, we were ready to leave at twenty past three. This was well within our schedule. We set out with Rog leading the way. The first two weirs were managed relatively easily; they were nothing worse than we had experienced many times before on our journey. Our first main hazard was at the third weir. We noticed Rog was heading for the centre of this weir. From our position some way behind, Dave and I agreed that the correct main channel was towards the left bank. Rog couldn't have changed his course in time even if we had shouted. As we expected, his canoe came to a sudden halt. Back-paddling frantically, Dave and I managed to stop ourselves also being drawn in. From our position we could only watch and hope that Rog would not capsize. He sat, trying to push his canoe off the rock on which he was ledged. All he managed to do was the worst thing possible: swinging the canoe around so that it was across the current. After this, capsize seemed even more difficult to avoid. Somehow, he managed to keep upright. He did the only thing possible: he abandoned ship. But this was not easy for him, because as soon as he lowered one leg over the side he was up to his waist in water. This made the job of getting his other leg out even more difficult as he attempted to maintain his balance. Obviously, Dave and I could not ask him to hurry up, but time was valuable to us. With his canoe still sideways, Rog dragged it to one side and gained a firmer foothold. He managed to turn the canoe again to face downstream. His problems were not over; he still had to get back in the canoe again. This was made difficult by the turbulent water and the very uneven riverbed. He threw caution to the wind, straddled his canoe, sat down and remained upright. What a relief!

Encouraged by a cheer from Dave and I, Rog found a safe passage over and beyond the weir. We followed: only to run aground. Dave and I had to get out and wade down for several yards. Somehow we achieved this and got back into our canoe without striking other obstacles or suffering damage. We realised we were falling behind schedule and could not afford to waste any more time.

On approaching the fourth weir, there was no decision about whether to line the canoes down or paddle through. We were faced with the most dangerous weir we had met on the river. The main current would certainly force a canoe onto several large rocks. There was no way of knowing what the

Tintern to Chepstow

Tintern Abbey with River Wye in the background

River conditions before setting off

Downriver from the Tintern camp

enormous waves flowing around them concealed. To have canoed on would have risked certain damage to our canoes. The exposed rocks made the rapids impossible to shoot through. Sadly, we could not take advantage of the tremendous speed of the water for it would have helped our progress downstream for some distance. Playing safe, we beached and lined the canoes down. This again proved difficult because of the force of the water but soon we were able to regain our seats in the canoes and paddle on.

We had been observed by men at a quarry on the left bank. This part of the river is rarely visited by canoeists because of the tidal influence and its dangerous conditions. We therefore attracted the attention of a large number of the quarry workers. Their works were at the top of the steep banks and many yards of it were lined by these men. They just stared in astonishment, most of them no doubt hoping we would capsize. They were to be disappointed, but they clapped us through and shouted ribald comments.

We were beginning to wonder if we would make Chepstow in time. We pressed on as fast as possible, as our target was still within reach if we met no more obstacles. Steady progress was made until we noticed the river's colour was changing to a rich red clay colour. The tide was flooding in and our progress downstream was cut drastically. The state of the water was very misleading; a tremendous bow wave created by the now oncoming torrent gave the impression of great speed. It was when we looked at the almost stationary riverbank alongside that we realised our true speed. We were paddling strongly but making little headway. Not wishing to give up with only three miles to go, we struggled on. The only way we could make any forward progress was to stay as close to the bank as possible; and wherever there was a bend keep to the inside, with the main current away from us. We met the real flood of the tide's surge at a large horseshoe bend in the river. We could not stop paddling, as we would have been forced back upstream immediately. We could not let our good work go to waste so we struggled on round the horseshoe bend. We were becoming exhausted as we inched forward against the upward flow. We had anticipated an easier cruise into Chepstow; nobody had forewarned us of the incredible power of the onrushing tidal wave.

Did we have the strength to keep going? Turning into the home straight into Chepstow we realised we were finished. We had to take a break, so we paddled to the near bank and held on to the security of some overhanging branches. Rog held on alongside us. We shared a bar of chocolate. We made an obvious decision: we would not be crossing the estuary today. Chepstow would now be our final target for the day. We knew we would undoubtedly have difficulties finding somewhere to camp for the night. Undeterred, we resumed paddling. After some minutes Rog, who was alongside us, said that he was going to have another piece of chocolate. He stopped paddling for a few seconds. In that time the force of the tidal water turned him full circle. By the time he recovered his stroke he was over a hundred yards behind us. It made us appreciate the phenomenal strength of the tide. Rog recovered his position behind us and we carried forward.

It was now raining heavily. We continued very slowly into Chepstow; gaining only two hundred yards every fifteen minutes. We reached the cliffs below Chepstow Castle and followed the muddy west banks downriver. Passing under a road bridge we rested at the only landing platform we could see with ladder steps leading up to dry land. It was half past five; we were exhausted. Where could we find sanctuary? We managed to get out and haul our canoes up the muddy steps onto firm ground.

Chepstow camp

View of Chepstow Bridge from our camp

Tintern to Chepstow

We were amazed how much water we tipped out of Rog's canoe; it had continued to leak and he was soaked through. It was now very cold and the rain was persistent.

We got out and hoped we could find somewhere to camp. We noticed a boatyard on the bank above us. There was a shelter which seemed attractive for cooking and drying out our soaked clothes. There would be room to put up just one of our tents on the muddy ground (the mud was regularly deposited by the tidal flood). We were wandering aimlessly around the boatyard when a lady came out from the nearby "Stuart House" and asked what we were doing. We told her of our epic journey from Tintern and our problem of finding a refuge for the night. To our delight she told us it would be alright to camp in the compound of the boatyard itself. The lady told us she was the wife of Eric Childs, a well-known Wye Fishery officer, and he was the manager/superintendent of the boatyard and the salmon fishery downstream. The method of fishing was unique she said; nets would be set across the Wye and controlled by Stop Boats.

After dragging the canoes up the slimy slipway, we were soon unpacking our canoes within the shelter of the boatyard. We set up one tent and prepared a hot comforting meal of beef stew. We ate well and relaxed. We chose to complete our recovery by retiring to the nearest public house (the "Lord Nelson") for the rest of the evening. In the pub we raised our pints. We had done one hundred miles down the Wye. It was a satisfying feeling; but we were concerned by our error in thinking that we could cross the estuary today.

Before closing time, we chatted to a local fisherman and explained the events of our day. He quickly explained where we had make our mistakes in the times of the tides and when we should have left Tintern to reach Chepstow. We should have left one hour at the turn of the tide BUT at the top of the tide on falling water NOT at low water with an incoming tide. Canoeing into Chepstow would have been easy and we would have avoided all the dangerous weirs. However, he also explained that even by doing this we could not have turned into the Severn and canoed upriver and across the estuary to the canal at Sharpness. The downstream flow of the Severn by then would have been too powerful for us to paddle against in our attempts to go upstream. We would most likely have been swept disastrously down to the Bristol Channel. He unnerved us by always describing the current in the estuary as the "boiling turbulence". His comments, however, didn't stop us from looking forward to continuing our adventure in the morning. We returned to the boatyard and the three of us settled comfortably into our tent.

It had been a long day.

Tintern to Chepstow

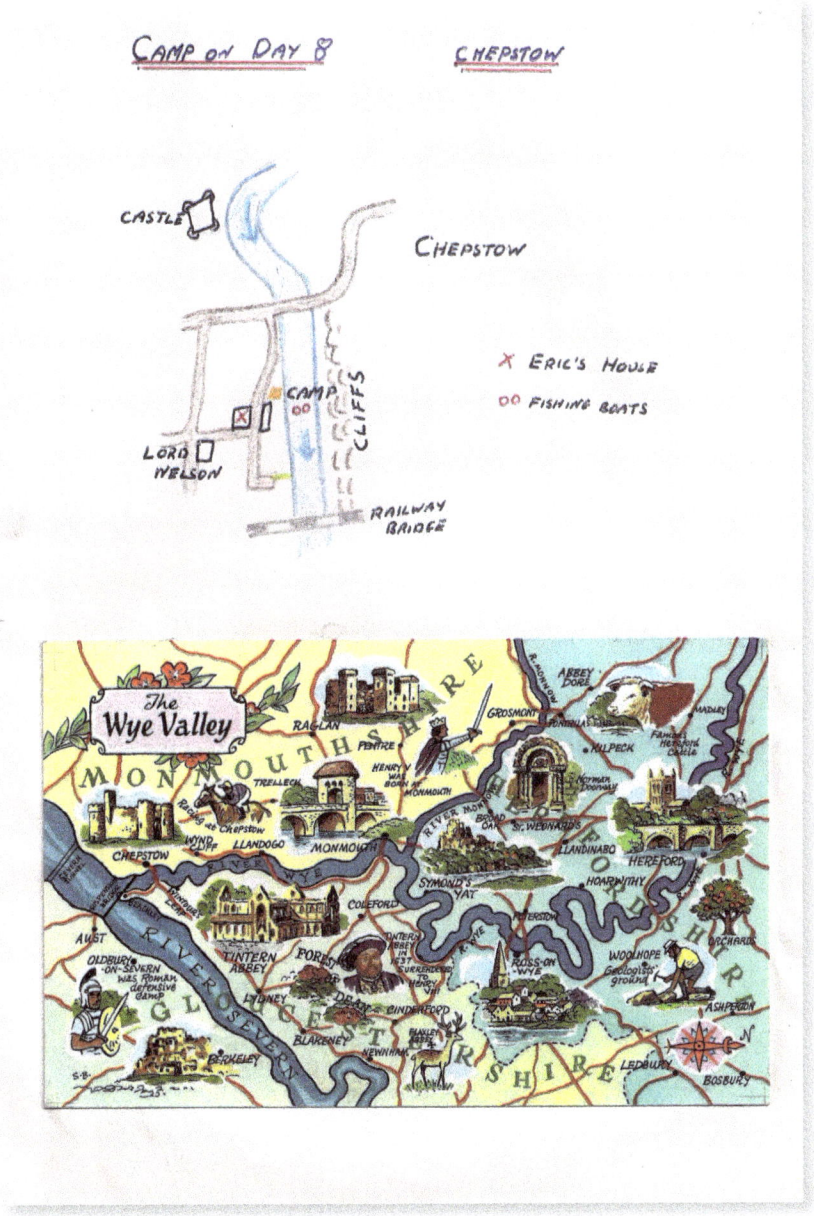

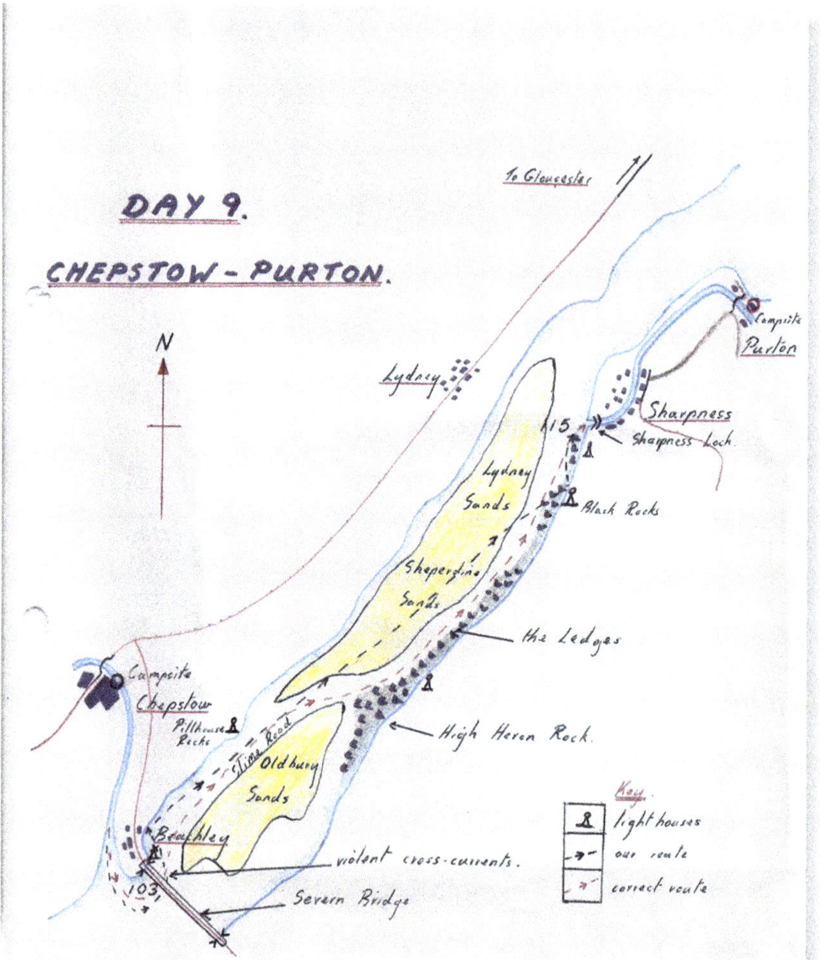

DAY 9.
CHEPSTOW - PURTON.

N

to Gloucester

Lydney

Sharpness
Sharpness Lock

15
Lydney Sands

Black Rocks

Sheperdine Sands

the Ledges

Campsite
Chepstow
Pillhouse Rocks

Stone Bend
Oldbury Sands

High Heron Rock

Beachley

violent cross-currents.

M 48

Severn Bridge

Campsite
Purton

Key:
- light houses
- our route
- correct route

Day Nine
Chepstow to Purton Bridges

Date: 23rd April 1967
Recorded by: David Hudson
Weather: overcast, becoming bright and hazy. Wind N.E.
River: very muddy with 40-foot drop of tide.
Severn Estuary: Three miles wide in places. Exposed sandbanks. Hazardous. Tide flowing in at six miles per hour.
Distance travelled: 15 miles

We finished breakfast by 10.30am. We chatted with Eric Childs and another man we referred to as "an Old Sea Dog" but we learned from Eric he was Captain William Groves. Apparently he lived in a house called "Riverside", the house next to an old iron bridge and opposite to the Bridge Inn. Eric informed us that Capt. Groves was an unsurpassed expert in the navigation of both the Severn and the Wye and he told us a story of Grove's prowess. On a July day in 1950 Capt. Groves took a party of members of the Chepstow Society on an excursion across the estuary to Clevedon in his vessel the "Firefly". The weather was not very good. When the time came to return to Chepstow a marked deterioration had set in and Capt. Groves warned the trippers it was going to be rough. At this, some of the less stalwart members of the party decided to make the return journey by train. As the more intrepid trippers were preparing to set out, some of the crew of a Campbell's Steamer which was moored near them left no-one in doubt that they thought it a foolish undertaking in so small a vessel in such severe conditions. A member of the Chepstow group, Mrs M Collins (a teacher and erstwhile Commandant of the Girls Training Corps), challenged their right to be called sailors if they feared a little rough weather – no matter the size of the vessel. However, despite the rain, wind and waves, they arrived back safely – albeit later than planned. They would have been wet and weary at Chepstow, no doubt as thankful to get ashore safely as we had been yesterday.

Captain Groves admitted to being in his seventies and the grand old sailor thrilled us with his tales of his voyages round the "Horn" in the old sailing ships. Although he was very experienced in the world's waters he rated the estuary of the Severn as the most treacherous. He was very informative about the time of the tides and the likely conditions we would encounter. We noted carefully his suggestions on what time to leave and what route to follow in the estuary. Even though he admired our spirit of adventure, he was concerned for our safety and warned us that we would encounter difficult conditions that warranted the greatest respect.

Undeterred, we went shopping for supplies and then took some photographs of our camp in the boatyard. The "Old Sea Dog" pointed out his boat the "Firefly" moored below us. We noticed it was the same vessel featured in a postcard we had bought in town showing Chepstow Castle and the River Wye at low tide conditions. We had a coffee and then packed our canoes ready for the off at 1.50pm.

Great difficulty was encountered launching the canoes due to thigh deep mud and a steep bank down to the river. We made use of a stair slipway which led to moored fishing boats, sliding the canoes down the steps. Carrying them would have been impossible due to their weight and us walking in the

The 'Old Sea Dog': Captain William Groves

Chepstow Castle, with the Captain Groves' 'Firefly' in the foreground

mud deposited on the steps by the fallen tide. The steps finished some twenty feet from the river. We had no alternative but to wade further into the mud and haul the canoes like sledges.

Once the canoes were in the water, we found we were so buried in the mud we couldn't pull ourselves up without capsizing our crafts. Dripping mud and slime, we hauled ourselves into one of the fishing boats. Here we splashed most of the mud from our legs. With our canoes alongside, we lowered ourselves into them. Rog was first away and we followed, but not before photographing a cargo vessel that was stranded way above the present level of the water.

With the strong flow of the river in our favour, we reached Beachley village at 2.30pm. On turning into the Severn – and a vast expanse of water it looked – we were surprised to see surf breaking in front of us. This indicated a sandbank to us but although we paddled backwards furiously it became obvious we couldn't avoid running aground. As the bows struck into the first wave we waited for the inevitable grinding halt.

Instead we sat amazed as the breaking water moved under us and into the mouth of the Wye. This was not water breaking on sand but the spearhead of an insurgent tide opposing the Wye's downstream flow.

Turning up the Severn, we paddled for twenty minutes to outrun the tide. We sought shelter by Chapel Rock. It was here we had been told we could wait while the initial fierce tide had its effects on the down rushing river. By 3.00pm the slack in which we rested became a tidal stream and we were rushed out into the pitching ooze.

Approaching the vast expanse of the Severn Bridge, we could see several people on the bridge watching our progress. This was stimulating but soon forgotten as we concentrated on the fast-flowing waters. Soon after passing under the bridge we ran into a turbulence of cross currents. We had underestimated the tide's strength; we were lucky to avoid the boiling sands and capsizing. Picking our course carefully, we moved out of the tidal flow and into calmer water on our left. Following the Sea Dog's advice, we beached beyond a disused ferry pier and prepared to sit out what we believed was the worst of the incoming tide.

Though it was sunny, a strong N.E. wind made it very cold and we sought shelter by some rocks. From this vantage point up the beach we had a wonderful view of the estuary. The yellow sandbanks were quickly covering over and the water surface was becoming choppy. The wind was in opposition to the S.W. flow of the tide and this conflict was producing a boil of brine. Anticipating that things would get calmer as the tide flowed further upstream, we continued our patient wait. The volume of water funnelling into the estuary caused us to return to the canoes and move them further up the beach. This action was necessary, even though initially we had carried the canoes some thirty feet from the water's edge.

Looking across the estuary towards the power station

The new Severn Bridge, viewed from our resting place

Our canoes did not have the benefit of spray decks, so we donned our lifejackets and – with them suitably inflated – we proceeded at 5.00pm further up a part of the estuary known as Slime Road. The tide was still gushing strongly and we were forced from the correct channel onto a surging cauldron of water over a recently submerged sandbank. It was alarmingly impossible to follow our tactic of staying close together. We could only hope to keep afloat and even this seemed highly improbable.

Jim and I, in our double canoe, were cast about like a cork and we had fears for the strength of the frame and canvas fabric of our fragile vessel. Everything was creaking under the strain and pounding from the tidal motion. At one point we felt that the surf would break our back. Far to our left we could see Rog battling to maintain his course. He seemed to be thrown further and further away from the top of one wave to another. Briefly he appeared almost airborne as a wave swirled and plunged under his slender craft.

Suddenly, in mid channel, we were aground on a sandbank; but quickly we were caught again by the flood tide and flung into deeper water. In those fleeting seconds, pictures had flashed before our eyes of the tankers that had fouled these sands and been pulverised by the pneumatic tide. For ten minutes we raced in calmer water and then entered further turbulence. Rog by this time had fought his way back to join us. We were far off course, but we aimed for buildings on the distant shore that we believed looked like the docks. Owing to the haze of confusion and spray, we were guided more by luck than judgement. Such was the speed of the tide that a buoy we aimed for, some 400 yards away, was missed by a full mile.

We beached at the "docks", only to find that we were not there at all but at the Power Station. We still had another two miles of canoeing to get to Sharpness Docks.

Jim located a fisherman and asked him for directions. Rog walked over to us, as he'd landed much further down the beach. This involved him crossing a small stream. Boldly stepping into the middle of the stream, he plunged chest deep into the freezing water. He found out the hard way that the stream was much deeper than he had imagined. With a few very choice words, he retraced his steps back to his canoe.

Having altered our bearings, we proceeded again towards the docks by closely hugging the north shore. Our nerves were challenged by an incoming tanker and the sight of a yacht floundering on a sandbank to our port.

On reaching the docks, we found we were required to wait while another tanker passed out from the lock. Holding our position was extremely difficult owing to the fast running current. Back-paddling proved futile, so we turned about. The drifting involved in turning meant furious paddling to avoid the jagged supports of the pier. It was impossible to hold any sort of headway against the tide, so we beached. Sitting in our canoes, we planned how to enter the lock. If we misjudged our run, the current would sweep us past the lock or we could be smashed into the pier. We decided to follow the tanker that was waiting downstream. This, we thought, would give us protection and also indicate the correct route. All the time the rising water was moving us off the shingle beach and trying to force us out. Strong paddling was necessary to nudge the bows of the canoes back onto land. After our already exhausting journey, it was very unnerving waiting there, but furious paddling was needed to maintain a position on land.

Thankfully we didn't have long to wait because the tanker, coming out of the lock, emerged and set off towards the Bristol Channel with her engines whining. She made slow progress against the tidal bore. The other tanker, the "Rosedale H" now made its run to the docks. When it reached the first pier, we moved out and followed. We narrowly avoided hitting the end of the pier and with our last remaining strength we forced our creaking craft between the piers, just missing the "Rosedale H" as she was manoeuvring into the open lock. We reached the safety of the lock and clung on to the tanker. We looked up and saw the incredulous faces of the crew and the waterways officials; their cameras much in evidence. Gradually, as the adrenaline subsided, we finished shaking and recovered our composure through controlled and relaxed breathing.

We had done it; we were safely across the estuary. We had staked our lives on a power that can never be built into an engine – the extra strength that men can always find within themselves when they know they must.

Chepstow to Purton Bridges

Cargo vessel at Low Water tide

Entering the Sharpness Canal

As the lock filled, Captain Burbidge, a British Waterways Official, called down to enquire if we were alright. Satisfied that we were OK, he asked to see our licences. We explained that we didn't have any as we'd hoped to buy them at the dock. Appreciating our tiredness, he told us to carry on to Gloucester and promised to ring through to Gloucester Docks to arrange for the licences to be prepared there for us rather than waste our time at Sharpness filling in forms. He was very enthusiastic but amazed about our crossing and said we could use his name for reference if anyone questioned our right to be on the canal. We asked him about available camping nearby and he suggested we try the inn at Purton. Rog reminded Captain Burbidge that he had written to him for directions across the estuary. He responded that he remembered the correspondence but he believed we would be crossing days earlier in powered craft and not in fragile canoes. Rog later recorded, in his diary, his thoughts on the crossing:

"The River Wye downstream from Chepstow had been successfully navigated in slack water and we entered the Severn Estuary to meet the force of the incoming tide. I recall facing one big wave and getting over it. This was the first surge of the famous Severn Bore, its strength increasing as the riverbanks narrowed some miles upriver. Together our two canoes turned left by Chapel Rock and we canoed uneventfully by the left bank and under the mighty Severn Road Bridge. As planned, we landed, beached the canoes, and waited for the right conditions before beginning our crossing to Sharpness Docks.

The Estuary, which seemed miles wide at this point, lay in front of us. We never doubted for a second that the crossing would cause us a problem, certainly not difficult or dangerous. However, watching the waters rising and the wind increasing, we were anxious to get started. We calculated we had nine miles or more to canoe across the vast expanse to the distant shore. Wearing shorts and thin clothing we found the wind bitingly cold. I was losing all feeling in my legs, my fingers were numb. We could not risk staying still any longer. We had to get going.

It soon became evident that we had totally underestimated the power of the tide. This was not going to be easy. Minutes into the journey our canoes were separated by the swirling currents; we were being forced further apart and in different directions. It was vital to watch the currents and waves; I concentrated intensely and the double canoe left my immediate field of vision. Although my focus was to keep bearing right to get to the other side meeting the waves head-on was desperately important. Just one wave taken sideways or any way off-centre could mean a capsize. It became a battle to go right after each wave then swing back to meet the next one. I remembered to resist the urge to keep pulling on the paddles and keep to the technique and style I had developed on the river; pushing forward like a boxer on the opposite paddle. But it was exhausting!

The increasing height of the waves made it difficult to see the now distant double canoe. Only at the crest of a wave was there a chance to glance over and catch sight of it. My canoe was riding the waves well but matters were complicated by the sudden swirling currents presumably created above the sandbanks below. The strength and speed of the tide was increasing and pushing me too straight and up the Estuary. It was now a major trauma fighting the force of the tide but trying still to tack to the right. It was becoming progressively more difficult to get across the fast-flowing central body of water. The physical effort was sapping my strength, but little by little I became more confident I was coping with the situation. I was hitting the top of each wave correctly without shipping any more water into the cockpit but I experienced one or two near capsizes when I was trying too hard to get in the right position between the swells and lows. My adrenaline was flowing. After what seemed like hours of this battering I was relieved to finally escape the fast central waters. I carefully paddled across to re-join Dave and Jim. We may have experienced elation at this point but I had more a feeling of relief;

we had made it across the Estuary and survived.

Still there was a final push to come; getting through those big docks into the Ship Canal. We shared an unspoken sense of achievement. Our adrenalin had given us a real confidence boost. It had taken grit, strength, stamina and endurance to get us this far; but if we could get this far we could do anything. Without doubt this had been an ultimate personal test of our ability to survive: and we had passed that test.

Yes, we had been alarmed at the conditions, but we just got stuck in and got through it. We never doubted we would not succeed. Each canoe had fought alone to cross the Estuary but I knew Dave and Jim in the double had experienced the same dangers and struggles as me. Was the additional strength of two people a more helpful factor as opposed to the greater manoeuvrability I had in the single? I could not imagine what it must have been like either in the front or in the back seat of their double canoe. They must have developed a strong teamwork to navigate the hostile waters and remain upright. But they had an advantage in being able to communicate with each other. Did they worry about me as I did about them? We had made no plans in advance for supporting either canoe in the event of a capsize. It would have been nigh on impossible to affect a rescue given the severity of the conditions. (Seagoing ships had recently foundered in these waters with the loss of life.) When we set off from the lee of the Severn Bridge we had assumed it would be possible to stay reasonably close together. As it was, conditions necessitated each canoe had to focus on surviving rather than staying together. Therefore, it was exhilarating to briefly share our experiences and marvel at getting across safely. We thought the main battle was won. So long as we could avoid being driven beyond and past the imposing entrance to the docks we would achieve our goal. Now all we faced was a secondary skirmish following a merchant tanker into the huge Sea Lock to be delivered safely into the calm and placid waters of the Gloucester and Sharpness Canal. Should not have been a problem, but it was."

Once out of the lock, a stop for a cigarette was a must. After some hasty intakes of nicotine, we reflected on our experience. We unanimously agreed that we were physically and emotionally drained, and that we had never been so frightened before. It was an experience we hoped never to repeat. (Most definitely we would not recommend anyone to copy it.) However, today's adventure was a truly magnificent achievement, one of which we are justly proud.

Two miles up the Sharpness Canal we came to Purton, our intended camp for the night. Permission was gained to use a field behind the "Berkley Hunt Inn". The landlord loaned us his milk trolley to tow the canoes into the field. Again we decided to use just one tent. After a delicious meat stew and tinned potato meal we retired to the inn for a much-deserved pint. We were introduced to the locals in the bar by the landlady. She explained what we had just achieved. They all thought us mad to have canoed that part of the river. One of the locals, who worked on the river, told us that a tanker had sunk three months previously with the loss of seven lives at exactly the point where we had gone aground on the sandbank. On fouling the sands, the tide had capsized the tanker. Such was the pounding it took, she broke her back. He thought us lucky not to have suffered the same fate. Others said we could easily have had the bottom ripped out of our canoes by the remaining wreckage. It was clear to us that we were with people who intimately knew the dangers of the estuary. Being praised for our courage and endeavour was humbling and more than ample reward for our ordeal. We returned to our tent, wrote up our diaries and settled down for a welcome sleep.

What a day!

Three Men in Two Canoes

Editor's note

On reflection, tackling the Estuary without spray covers to keep water out of the canoes seems, at best, highly risky, and at the worst foolhardy. I can't remember them being available to us; either that, or in our naïve ignorance, we believed them unnecessary. Also, our canoes were without any buoyancy aids. We donned lifejackets but they would not have kept our heads above water if we were unconscious. Although we had done desk-based research on our route, we were massively unaware of the dynamics of the Estuary and the dangers we could face. We had no concept that the power of the tide would be impossible to canoe against, and we could be so helpless and at its mercy. We did not understand the different directions the water was surging or realise its speed could vary in various areas across the estuary. We should have studied charts and the times of tides far more closely. A close inspection of the Estuary from the riverside or off the bridge (on different days with different weather conditions) would have aided our planning. But hindsight is a wonderful thing. If we had seen the Estuary, and its dangers previously, it is certain we would not have gone anywhere near it.

An endless number of worrying questions can now be posed: What were the contingency plans? Was it ever possible to pull out at any stage? If either canoe got into difficulty or capsized what were the plans for help, survival or rescue? Were the canoes designed to be strong enough for those conditions? How could we get water, shipped into the canoe, bailed out? How long could a canoe stay afloat without buoyancy? What could happen if we were swept upstream beyond the docks? Who knew where we were and what we were doing? The list goes on and on, but, as mentioned elsewhere, Health & Safety and Risk Assessment were both unheard of in 1967.

Chepstow to Purton Bridges

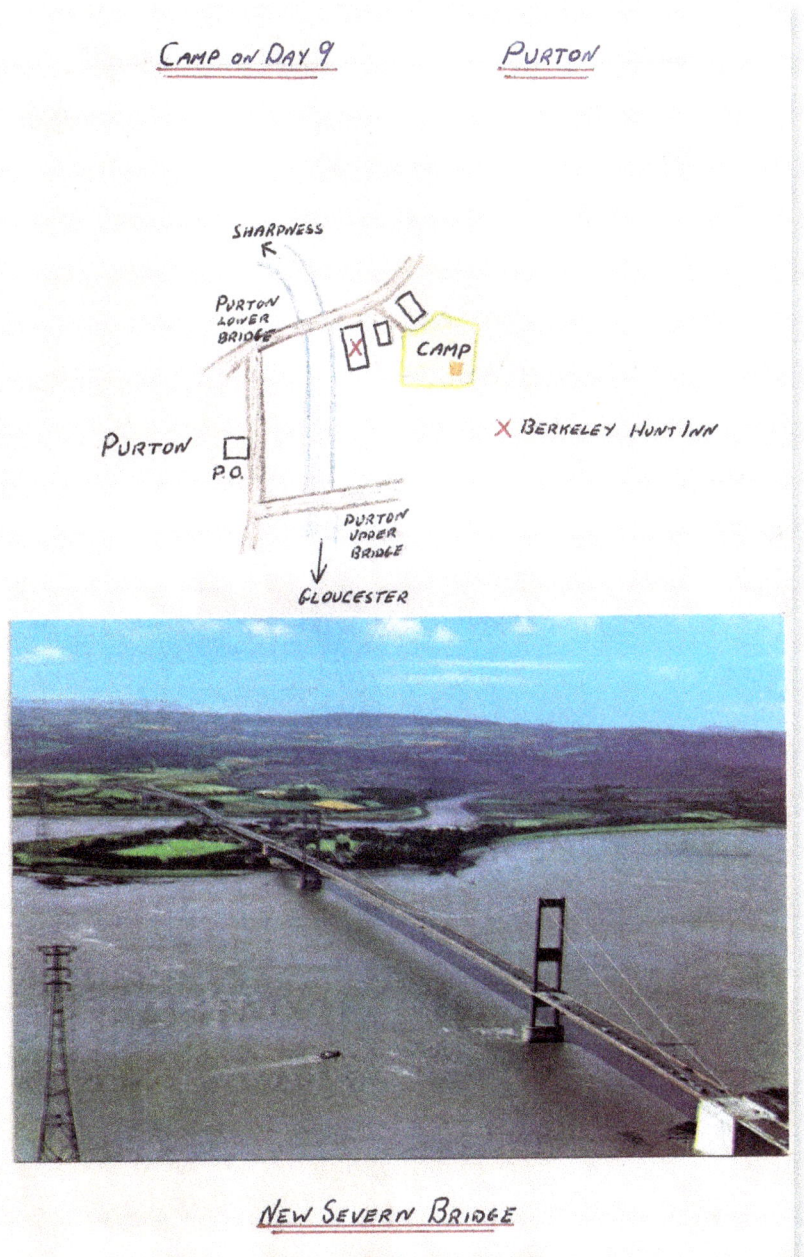

DAY 10

PURTON BRIDGES - WAINLODE

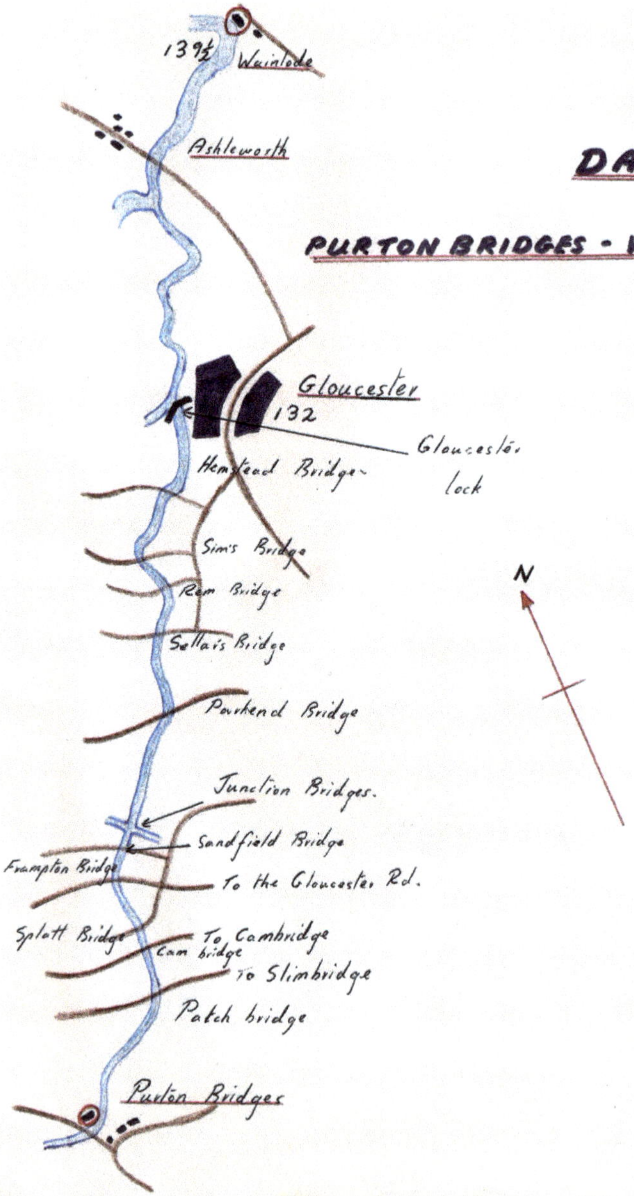

139½ Wainlode

Ashleworth

Gloucester
132
Gloucester lock

Hemstead Bridge

Sim's Bridge

Rea Bridge

Sellars Bridge

Parkend Bridge

Junction Bridges

Sandfield Bridge

Frampton Bridge

To the Gloucester Rd.

Splatt Bridge

To Cambridge
Cam bridge
To Slimbridge

Patch bridge

Purton Bridges

N

Day Ten
Purton Bridges to Wainlode

Date: 24th April 1967
Recorded by: Roger Annable
Weather: cold, dull and rainy – becoming a little brighter.
Canal: dead water with long straight stretches, occasionally interrupted by very low swing-bridges. River Severn: deceptively strong flow against craft travelling upriver; deep, muddy and uninteresting
Distance travelled: 24 miles

Didn't get an early start. Overslept after previous day's ordeal to rise at 9.30am and cook a good breakfast. Dave and Jim broke camp while I went across the bridge to the village shop to collect provisions. The shop seemed to be the village meeting place, for inside were several of the locals we had met last night. Again they were very friendly, talking freely and easily, asking more questions. Apparently we were the village heroes for the day.

After loading the canoes, we finally left Purton at 12.55pm. We proceeded up the Gloucester and Berkley Ship Canal slowly in rainy conditions, cautiously avoiding the swell (which was sometimes considerable) of incoming barges. Getting no help, of course, from the near-static water, we slogged away towards Gloucester.

Passing under swing-lock bridges often necessitated

ducking down low and removing headgear since clearance was only two-to-three feet. The trip into Gloucester was hard work and not particularly interesting. In fact, the only entertainment was provided by a young dirty swan which we encountered on the canal just above the Severn Wild Fowl Trust at Slimbridge: it swam about twenty yards in front of us all the way to Gloucester, occasionally 'taking off' to maintain its lead. If only I could have lassoed it and used its strength to tow me into Gloucester.

One mile from the Gloucester, we had to pause at the canal side while a large naval vessel, HMS Soberton M1200, moved slowly by us. It had been paying a courtesy visit to Gloucester, and was now being towed by a tug towards the Severn Estuary at Sharpness. As we paddled alongside a nearby dredger, a group of its workmen, who were taking time off to watch the navy departing, pointed down to our two canoes beneath them. "Look!" said one, "he's taken his cap off so he won't have to salute." Amused by this comment, we waited patiently until the way was clear and I could again don my army cap and proceed.

Giving way to the naval vessel HMS Soberton M1200

Editor's notes on the Soberton: I posted our picture of HMS Soberton on the Forces Reunited website and it drew this response from Colin Goodwin: "I was one of the two Radio Operators on board and remember that trip well. We were feted by the Mayor and his Council and played them at Skittles in a 'can't remember' hostelry. The other Radio Operator was Barry Davies and the skipper Lt James Weatherall. He went on to become Admiral Sir James Weatherall and commanded HMS Ark Royal when they filmed the Documentary for TV. He was also the Admiral of the Sea Cadets and Captain of the Diplomatic Corps. I remember seeing canoeists during our transit of the Sharpness Canal. I am almost certain the figure on the deck is me."

A quarter of a mile before Gloucester Lock we stopped to buy chocolate and fruit pies at a shop by the side of the canal. Once out of the canoes we realised how cold it was, as the cold wind whipped around our bare legs. We were over-exposed for these cold conditions, only wearing swimming shorts. We stood shivering in the street as we refuelled ourselves for the second stage of our journey. Upon resuming, our friend the dull swan was still paddling in front of us, but not for long. As we approached the lock at Gloucester the swan was attacked by other swans that drove it squawking behind some vessels anchored at the side. A Waterways official hailed us from the dock wall high above us, enquiring whether we were travelling with the army or as individuals. If we were travelling with the army, he explained, lock fees could be referred to our commanding officer. After some frivolous deliberation we decided not to reply with the name of our Head of P.E. Dept. "Major J Osborne, 242 Flaxley Road, Birmingham 33". The official informed us that in ten minutes a barge was coming through the lock in the opposite direction and we could proceed into the lock as soon as it had left. So we moored our craft at a landing stage and entered

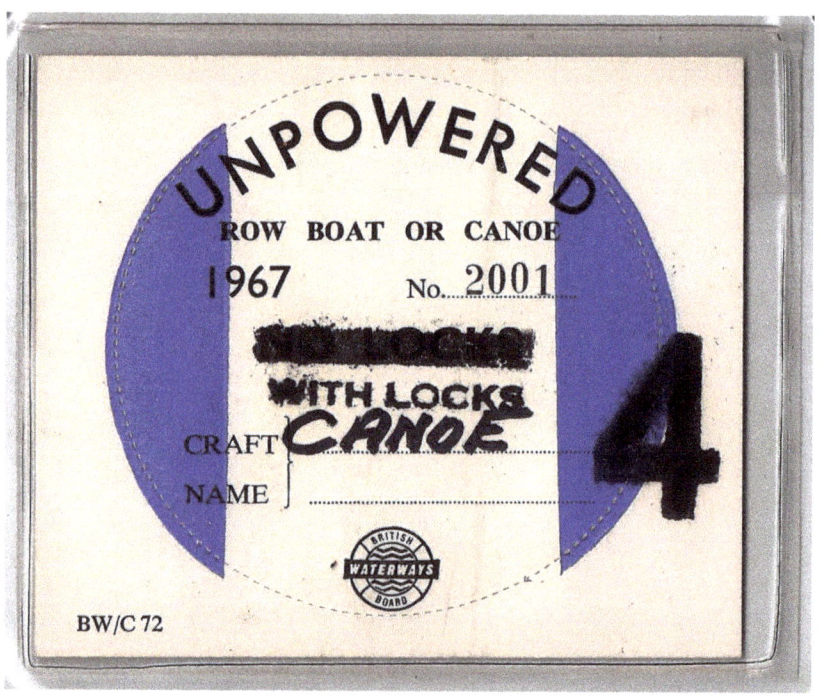

Our lock tickets for the route home.

Our British Waterways licence for the Ship Canal.

a warm dry cabin occupied by the white peak capped official. We paid our fees and waited for the appropriate time for our entry into the lock.

The officer was amazed at our trip and the fact that we had even attempted to cross the estuary at this time of the year on a Spring tide. Anything over 26 feet, he quoted, was extremely dangerous and last night's tide had been measured at 30 feet 6 inches. He himself had seen tugs and larger craft struggling desperately in such conditions. He informed us that Captain Burbidge had phoned through from Sharpness Docks telling him to expect our arrival. Having paid our lock fees, which totalled an extortionate 30 shillings altogether, we paddled into the lock after the barge had passed through. As the level of the water gradually fell, hundreds of little elvers were left clinging to the sides of the lock, showering us from time to time from above when they fell. Soon the gates were open and we passed through them into the River Severn.

At this point Dave, known to be an expert on statistics, provided us with some interesting points about our journey so far. We had conquered the second highest tide in the world on the second highest tide measured so far this year. Also, we had canoed the length of the second largest ship canal in the country and we were now on the second longest river in the British Isles.

The going was quite difficult as we began paddling up the Severn. There were no rapids and little evidence of a main current but certainly there was a definite flow against us which could be easily detected by the slow rate at which the banks went by. Few landmarks or anything of interest were to be seen, thus making our upstream struggle even more laborious. Having previously agreed that Wainlode would be the day's target, we continued paddling. But we didn't arrive until 9.10pm in fading light. Very tired, we moored just above the line of sunken craft which formed the shape of a crescent on the East side of the river. We sought permission to camp at the nearby "Red Lion Inn".

Permission to camp on the riverbank was gained as a short rainstorm broke out. We set up camp and unloaded in the darkness. Again we decided to use only the one tent. A Vesta Chicken Curry meal was cooked inside the tent and thoroughly enjoyed by all of us. By this time, we had donned extra clothes for warmth. The washing up completed, we were too exhausted to venture out of the tent (even for a drink in the local inn) and so settled down for a good night's sleep on the banks of the river. But we were constantly disturbed by a conglomeration of elver fishermen with their revving cars, searchlights, nets and transistor radios as they worked the east bank for the harvest of thousands of elvers that were moving upstream. We soon realised that our camping position was slap bang in the middle of a famous hotspot for elvers in this area. It didn't look promising for a quiet night.

Tomorrow we hope to go "elver leather". We went well today, with twenty-one and a half miles paddled in poor conditions.

Hope to get an early start in the morning.

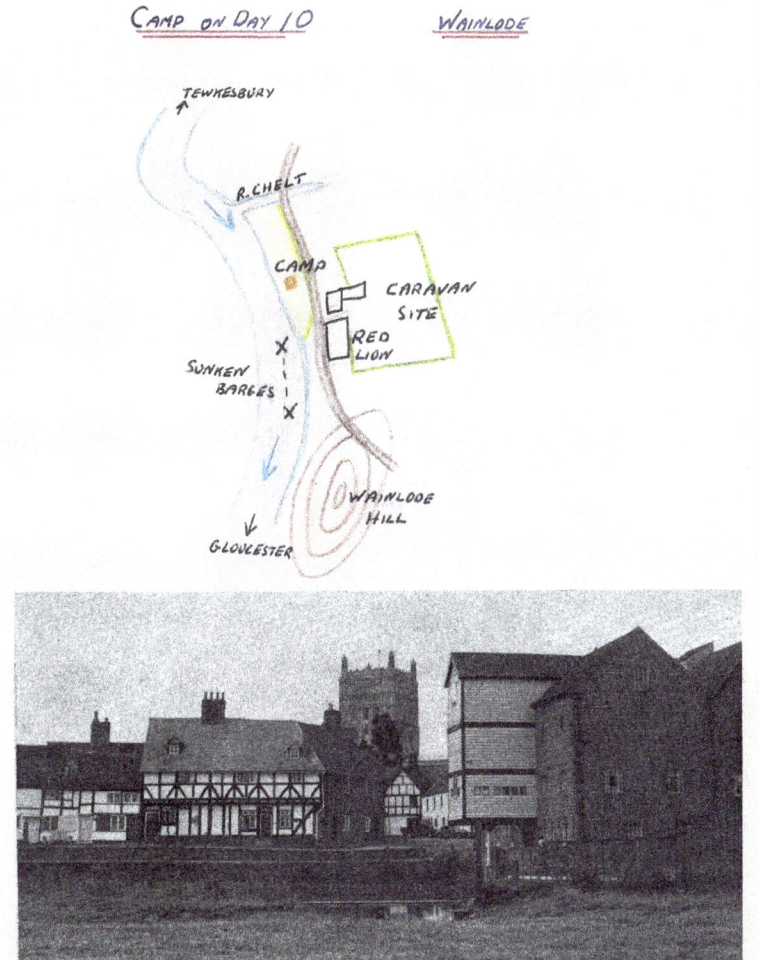

DAY 11.
WAINLODE - KETCH HOTEL

A38
Campsite
160 Ketch Hotel
yacht club.

Sandy point

Severn Stoke Wharf

Upton on Severn — Upton Bridge — tanker wharf
Saxon's Lode
Motorway bridge
M50

Mythe bridge
145½ Tewkesbury Lock
Tewkesbury
Mill Avon
Cheltenham Colleges Boat-House

Haw Bridge
Wainlode Campsite
139½

N

Day Eleven
Wainlode to Ketch Hotel below Worcester

Date: 25th April 1967
Recorded by: R 'Jim' Murton
Weather: overcast, wind at first becoming calm. *River:* very wide and dirty
Distance travelled: 21 miles

Today history was made: we started canoeing before eleven o'clock; in fact it was five minutes to eleven. Whilst loading the canoes we were surprised to see that the tide was still affecting the river. We were grateful that it would be in our favour in our journey into Tewkesbury. Obviously, the tide was not very powerful but we would appreciate any help as the very blustery wind was against us all the way. We set out and found we still had to work hard to make any appreciable headway. We had covered about two and a half miles into Tewkesbury when we sighted a tanker coming down the river. We pulled over to the right to let it pass on the correct side. As it came nearer we all agreed it looked familiar; it was. It turned out to be the "Rosedale H" – the tanker we had followed into Sharpness Docks. On seeing us, the crew lined the decks and gave us a hearty cheer and wished us good luck. This encounter gave us much encouragement as we continued on our way.

When Tewkesbury Lock came into view, Rog started working his bicycle horn frantically as he had always done on approaching locks. Dave and I did not like to see him making

The Rosedale H (archive photo)

a spectacle of himself, but it kept him happy. (We knew that all ships should sound their horns on approaching locks; Rog was convinced that this rule applied to canoes as well.) I got out at the lock and showed the lock keeper our licences. He had received a telephone message from the keeper at Gloucester who had obviously told him of our exploits. He also was astonished about our journey. However, he did mention that the previous keeper anticipated we would reach Tewkesbury Lock before eleven o'clock.

Passing smoothly through the lock we started looking for a place to land so that we could go into Tewkesbury for a midday snack and buy some provisions. Paddling towards the bank, we passed some GPO men working there. They suddenly started laughing heartily. We thought they were just laughing about our appearance, but it proved to be more than that. They all dispersed for a few seconds and then reappeared holding great sods of earth. These they duly hurled at us; no direct hits but near enough to drench us with spray. (If only we could have summoned up a squadron of Mute Swans to make a silent bombing raid on them.) Sadly, all we could hurl at them were some choice and colourful comments. Anyway, they had amused us and helped brighten up our day.

We enjoyed a break in the town, although Rog was worried about the affect his military cap might have on the many army personnel we encountered there. (But he managed to escape without being apprehended and court-marshalled for his appearance.) Supplies bought, we were soon on our way again. The tide now had no effect on slowing the downstream flow of the Severn. It became a slog into the town of Upton Upon Severn. Progress was discouragingly slow as we looked ahead at the long straight stretches of water in front of us. On reaching Upton, our slow progress forced us to change our planned day's itinerary. We could no longer reach our intended campsite of Bevere Island. To go on would have meant canoeing for over an hour in darkness. This would have been ridiculous, especially as we were not assured of a campsite on arrival at Bevere. Consequently we changed our destination to a supposed campsite by the Ketch Hotel, thus cutting five miles off our original itinerary. The miles to the Ketch seemed equally arduous; it was evident we were becoming stale from such a sustained programme of boring upriver canoeing. At one stage I had to cheer up the lads with my brilliant wit. It is unfortunate, but I don't think Dave and Rog would agree with my last remark.

On reaching the Ketch, there was a caravan site which made us think that camping would also be allowed. We approached a man who was working on a moored boat, but he said that camping was certainly not allowed on the site itself but he didn't think that anyone would mind if we used the adjacent field. We thanked him and found a suitable place to moor up. Rog went to inspect the field. To our surprise he said it looked almost impossible to find a place to erect a tent. Dave and I couldn't

Arriving at The Ketch at dusk

believe this and went to look for ourselves. The vegetation in most parts was three feet high. Not wishing to do any more canoeing, we found a spot where the undergrowth was only two feet high. After trampling the ground for many minutes, we managed to erect one tent. We were just about to fill the tent with our equipment when we spotted an ominous angry-looking figure striding towards us. He told us that he could not allow us to camp in the field as it had just been bought by the caravan site owner and consequently it was private land. The only suggestion he could make was a field on the opposite side of the river. Not wishing to move, we began hinting about how early we would be leaving the next morning. He slowly gave in and said he would pretend not to have seen us, provided that we were gone before nine o'clock the next day. He then stopped for several minutes, chatting about the river and saying that we could accompany him to his house for our water supply. Feeling very relieved, we completed the unpacking, cooked a tasty stew and potato meal, and retired to the Ketch for a drink. In the hotel we weighed up the possibility of completing our project the following day. We decided unanimously that it could be done, especially with an early start being forced upon us.

Wainlode to Ketch Hotel below Worcester

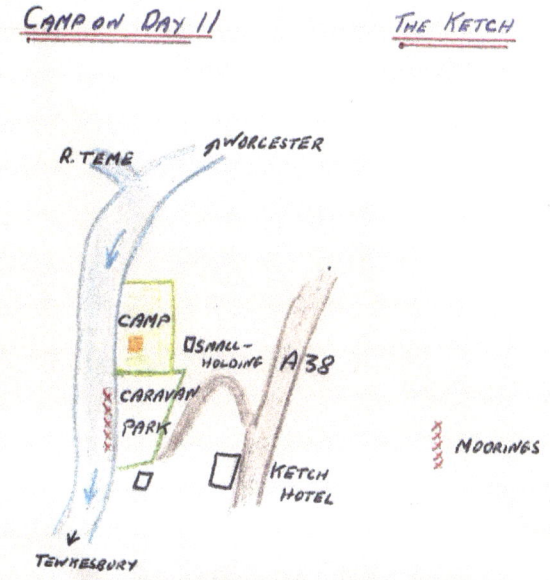

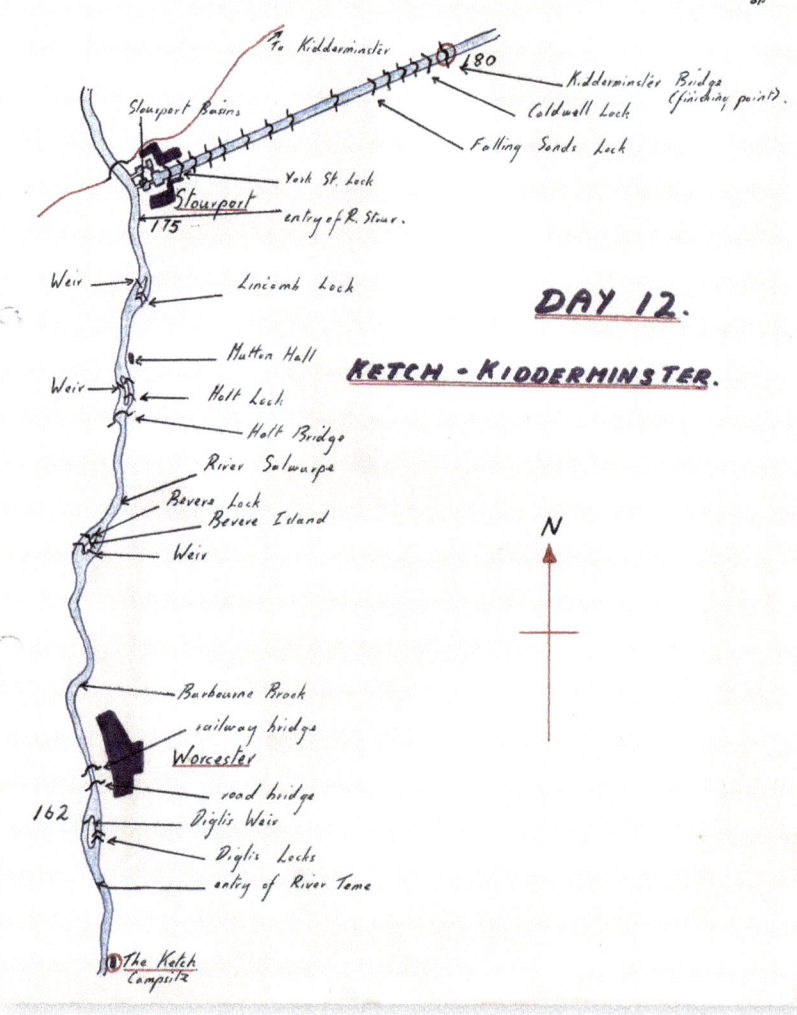

Day Twelve
Ketch Hotel to Kidderminster

Date: 26th April 1967
Recorded by: David Hudson
Weather: sunny, becoming overcast, light breeze. *River:* sluggish, deep.
Canal: filthy, much rubbish
Distance travelled: 20 miles

Following the smallholder's advice, we were up early this morning. Leaving the site without trace of our presence, we set off at 10.30am: our earliest start of the voyage. Diglis locks were reached by 10.50am and Jim decided to film our two canoes entering and leaving the lock.

Worcester Bridge was reached by 11.30am and we took the opportunity to stretch our legs. Ignoring the remarks and glances of onlookers, we walked into town and bought some postcards and chocolate. Rog made a phone call to his girlfriend at Summerfield College, Kidderminster, to arrange a rendezvous by the canal in Kidderminster later in the evening.

Leaving at 12.10pm we paddled non-stop to Bevere Island and its lock, a distance of three and a half miles. Refreshment was taken in the Camp Inn. Here we reviewed our prospects of reaching Kinver today. We felt that if we reached Stourport by 5.00pm we could do the canal to Kinver comfortably in three to four hours.

Passing through Bevere Lock at 2.10pm, we put our heads down and paddled without a pause for an hour.

Roger films the river as Jim dismantles our camp at The Ketch

Roger entering Diglis lock at Worcester

Approaching Worcester Cathedral

During this long slog we somehow managed to cover four miles. This brought us to Holt Fleet Lock. The lock keeper wasn't present. Jim went in search of him and found him by the weir fishing for salmon. On seeing Rog, in his now infamous RAMC Captain's cap, the lock keeper remarked that he looked like Monty leading a patrol into battle. As we moved out of the lock the keeper called out to Jim: "Look after the Brigadier, we might need him for the next war!"

After a pause for cigarettes, we embarked on another four-mile stint. This was an exhausting hour. As we struggled to maintain our upstream progress against the deceptive current we met a party of school canoeists travelling downstream. The master in charge remarked on the ease of the paddling. So it should have been: he was going downstream.

After Lincomb Lock, we hastily completed the remaining one and a quarter miles of our trek up the Severn that brought us to Stourport. As planned, we had made the entrance to the Staffs and Worcs canal by 5.00pm. Here we received a setback. The lock keeper had decided that the lock, which controlled

Ketch Hotel to Kidderminster

Arriving at Stourport-on-Severn

the entrance to the canal basin, would be closed until 6.00pm. This was contrary to Waterway Regulations but there was nothing we could do to alter the situation. Speaking to boat owners while we waited, we learned that this lock keeper had established a terrible reputation and there have been many attempts to have him removed. When he charged us the exorbitant price of fifteen shillings for a lock key, we had further reason to understand the stories told about him.

6.00pm saw us waiting to be let into the basin; and waiting and waiting. At 6.45pm the lock keeper finally arrived obviously the worse for having partaken of copious liquid refreshment. He ordered us to hurry up as he was about to close the basin for the night. This flagrant abuse of rules and regulations caused our tempers to rise and we let fly with some appropriate choice comments. He was totally unmoved by our "complaints" for we had neither influence nor affluence to sway his actions.

It was now obvious to us we couldn't reach Kinver by nightfall, but we pressed on hoping at least to fulfil our obligations to those waiting for us at Kidderminster. The canal was filthy with vegetable waste and wood scrap. Stakes, presumably thrown in by children, protruded in many places and our progress was slowed by us having to avoid obstructions and steer a safe passage. At Falling Sands Lock, we in the double canoe came to a grinding halt on a submerged log. How the canoe was not holed is a mystery, for it created a four-foot graze under the bows.

Such was our haste in failing light that when the two canoes were in the lock I flooded the chamber too quickly. The flush of water whipped up the detergent properties of the water and the foam it created totally engulfed Rog in his canoe. Had he not been using his chinstrap he would have lost his cap.

With darkness now on us, we reached the outskirts of Kidderminster at Caldwell Lock. We were delighted to see Rog's girlfriend Linda on the towpath. She had brought two of her college friends along to meet us. Our dishevelled appearance certainly suggested to them the enormity of our expedition. We had much to tell them but it was amazing how light-heartedly we recalled our experiences and hardships.

Paddling up the Staffordshire & Worcestershire Canal in near-darkness

Ketch Hotel to Kidderminster

With the girls walking the towpath alongside us we paddled the quarter mile to the bridge carrying the main road into Kidderminster. It was too dark to continue safely and we had no provisions or finances for another camp. And we were exhausted. We had reached the end of the journey; all 180 canoed miles of it. I had no alternative but to find a public phone box and phone my father to ask him to come and pick us up and transport us back home.

We were very disappointed that we couldn't complete the final six miles. But there was no other choice in the circumstances. After what we had been through, we felt there was no disgrace in accepting a lift by car for the remaining leg back to our starting point of Kinver.

Now we could relax. Jim and Rog will return to their homes tomorrow. On Friday we will return to Saltley. Each of us is looking forward to telling of our experiences to our P.E. colleagues and discovering what they did for their adventures. We just hope that Jim's car will start in the morning.

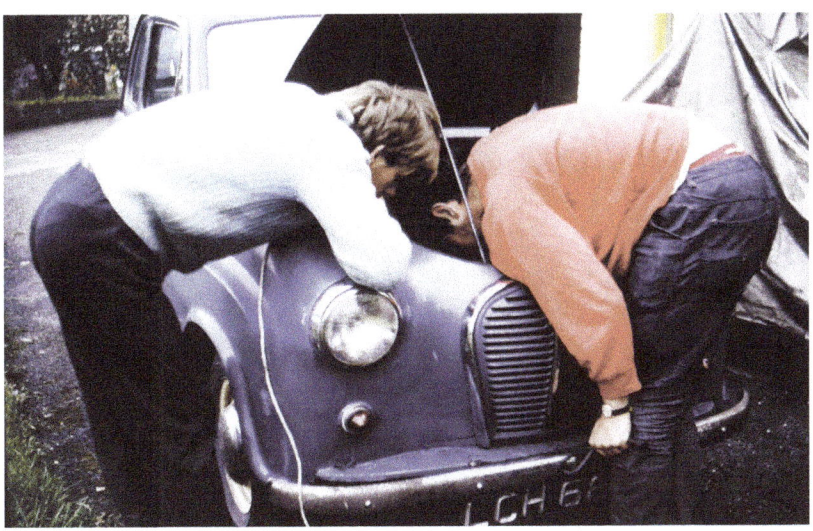

We hoped that Jim's car would start. It didn't!

Post-adventure

Return to College

The next day we were thrilled to return to Saltley and find out what our fellow P.E. students had done for their Expedition Adventure. Naturally we were excited to tell them of our success. It soon became obvious that not all of our colleagues wanted to discuss what they had accomplished. They were writing up their accounts and were keeping their cards close to their chests. Everyone was hoping for a good assessment and didn't want to give anything away. Had they embarked on their adventure with the same enthusiasm and success as us?

Gradually we uncovered some of the rumoured anecdotes of their adventures:

Three of our talented long-distance runners had hoped to run from John O'Groats to Land's End: a distance of 1,000 miles. Apparently, injuries cut the run very short and they completed most of the route by car; only being able to hobble into a few of the towns on their route with a collecting bucket for charitable donations.

One of our most gifted left-sided natural footballers chose to undertake an adventure on his own. He claimed that he got distracted and didn't actually do anything. So he wrote up a totally fictional account of three days in the wild.

Three of our most talented First Team football players chose to visit a few Midland football grounds, soak up their ambiance, partake of a few beers and camp nearby. Their account read well. What joy!

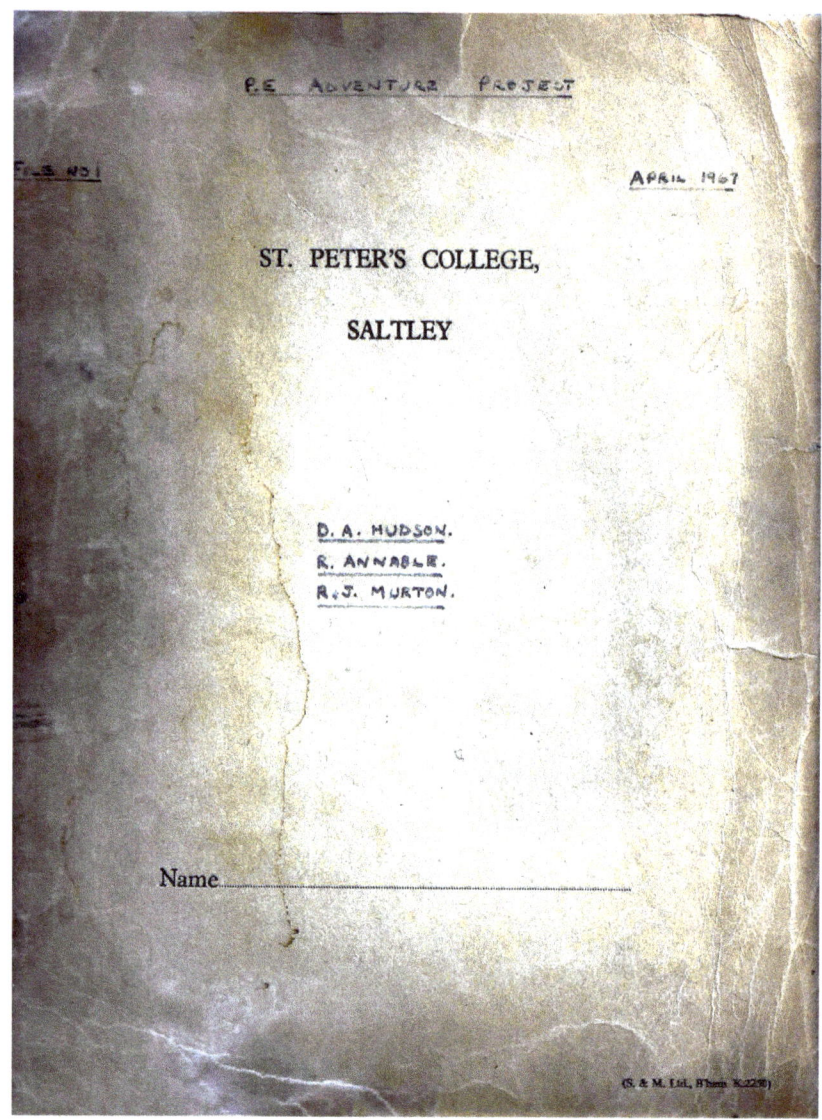
Cover from the original log of the adventure.

a large rapid. The island below Symonds Yat divides water L into a rapid. This is deep and straight, but has waves large enough to curl into the cockpit. We watched father and son deal competently with this hazard and then rushed back to our canoes for our attempt. Our haste was caused by the cold and the stench from a dead sheep. Reg worried for his life dons lifejackets and gives Tim his cine camera and a description of his blue shorts. Tim offered the advice "You'll be alright, you'll get over it!" It's a good job he did for again he was carrying the food. A dead cow floating down the rapid proved an unusual obstruction to avoid.

A mile downstream we reached our intended campsite at the Forestry Commission campsite. Although it was 5·30 p.m. the warden was nowhere to be seen. Undeterred we waited by a wood fire left by the occupants of a previous camp. Having pulled the warden missing after a second search we set up camp and enjoyed a beef curry. This campsite has all modern amenities and is set in a picturesque wooded valley. It caters for school and scout groups. It could provide a perfect site for any school camp.

Looks like an early night for a change. Hope for an early start in the morning. Tintern Abbey should prove interesting and who knows, with our beards, we may get enrolled!

Internal page from the original log of the adventure.

Our rugby stalwarts were more successful. They recounted a trip to the Lake District. They arrived in the dark and managed to persuade the landlord of a pub to let them pitch their tent in the pub grounds. Apparently one of them woke in the night due to a nightmare; they put it down to eating too much cheese. They didn't remember much of what they did over the weekend, except to listening to Keith Jarrett scoring a fabulous try for Wales against England at the Cardiff Arms Park. The Welsh gloated and the English sulked.

Others reported that their P.E. adventure was a waste of time and they abandoned it after a couple of nights. One or two told us nothing. Some said they would tell us what they had done in due course; possibly they were trying to bluff us.

We ignored all their negative comments and concentrated on writing up the account of our adventure.

We divided up the twelve days of the trip between us; each writing up four days into longhand. Jim contributed the maps; I drew diagrams of our campsites; Rog did the editing and composition of our final account and compiled a folder containing the maps, guides, postcards and information booklets we had accumulated during the journey. Eventually the colour slides and cine films were returned to us after processing by Kodak; we were pleased with their quality and included them in Rog's evidence folder. Three weeks after completing our canoeing adventure I handed our written account to P.E. tutor Steve Allatt for assessment. He accepted our invitation to view the cine film on Rog's projector and quickly gave us positive comments. Hopefully he would also favourably assess our Log.

A week later Steve returned the Log with his written assessment:

"This is a first-rate log of what was an extraordinary achievement. You are to be congratulated on a superb performance. The illustrations and slides are very good indeed. My only criticism is your failure to summarise what you felt were the educational values of such an undertaking. The quality of the rest of the work and the undoubted merits of your expedition, however, enable me to overlook this omission."

GRADE 'A' – C.S. Allatt

We could not have been more pleased with our grade and his encouraging words. We soon discovered our log was the most highly graded of all those submitted by our P.E. colleagues.

And as to "the educational values of such an undertaking"? That was easy: we had lived to tell the tale!

Post-Saltley Reunions

After leaving college in July 1967, the contact between Dave, Rog and Jim declined due to their geographical disparity and their lives going in different directions. Jim and Dave, with Dave's fiancée Lynn, attended Roger's marriage to Linda in London in 1968. Roger and Jim attended Dave's wedding to Lynn in Kinver 1970. Roger and Linda went off to teach in the Bahamas in 1971. Jim visited Dave and Lynn in 1972. There was a brief exchange of Christmas cards for a few years and then nothing between them until 2013 when Dave rediscovered the log of their canoe adventure in his attic. He set about transcribing it with the intention of sending copies to Rog and Jim. But he did not know where they lived.

 A stroke of luck, or call it Fate, intervened. Dave met Robert and Janet Lines on an art course in Mid-Wales. In conversation they disclosed they were retired teachers; Dave from Kinver in Staffordshire and the Lines originally from Cleobury Mortimer in Shropshire but now living at Devil's Bridge in Ceredigion. Dave told them that friends of his, Roger and Linda Annable, had taught in Shropshire. Amazingly, Janet had taught with Linda in the same Cleobury primary school and they were still in regular contact. She gave Dave the Annable's address in Whitstable, Kent where he could contact them and send them the log.

 The search for Jim proved more difficult. Lynn, Dave's wife, used her skills as a genealogist to track him down. She found records for a marriage between a Roger J Murton and

Margaret Belcher in Leicestershire in 1978. Further research discovered the birth to them years later of a daughter Beth. Lynn consulted Facebook on the Internet for any Beth Murton listed. The results featured a Beth Murton studying for a Physiology degree at Bristol University. One of her photographs showed her with her father. He was bald and with a moustache; obviously not the Jim Dave remembered. Lynn was certain it was Jim: "Forget the bald head and moustache, just look at the eyes, it has to be him." Dave sent a request to Beth saying he was trying to contact an old college friend and was she related to Roger 'Jim' Murton who was with him at Saltley from 1964-67. She did not reply.

Undeterred, Lynn Googled "Margaret Murton" and eventually discovered the website of a prominent artist living in Leicestershire. Her biography stated she was married to Roger a craftsman in furniture mostly involved with the design and making of contemporary pieces. This didn't look too promising but Margaret had a contact link on her website and Dave sent his details asking if she was related to Roger whom he knew from Saltley. Within hours, Dave got a reply: from Jim. Yes, he was the Roger married to Margaret, and Beth was their daughter. (She had missed Dave's email as it went straight to her spam folder.) Dave now had the Murton's address in Ashby de la Zouch and he could send Jim the log.

Jim was the first to acknowledge, by email, receiving the transcribed log. "Many thanks for making such an effort to find me. Like you, and no doubt Roger Annable, I am still reminded of that fabulous experience. I had no idea where the log was – I thought it may have been left at college. The fact that you have it and have taken the trouble to transcribe it is great news. Wow! What a document – it really transported me back to an amazing experience. I don't think at the time that we realised what we had achieved. Thank you so much for transcribing it. Margaret and Beth have both read it and were suitably impressed. Mind you I am now hearing the occasional "Jim" being used to call me from the garden or somewhere else in the house. I will try to locate my slides; the last time I saw them they seemed to have deteriorated – either that or we completed most of our journey shrouded in mist.

There were so many incidents that I had completely forgotten about – yes, it was a wonderful dose of nostalgia. When I return from holiday in Cornwall next week I will contact you and arrange a meeting. Perhaps a pub lunch at a venue between us?"

Roger's email arrived the next day. "What a surprise. We have just returned from holiday to find a very interesting parcel containing your transcribed log which drew immediate smiles and laughter from both Linda and myself. Well done and thanks for getting it together and sending it to us. I've read the Estuary chapter three times and cannot believe what we tackled and completed: neither can my daughter who is both amused and intrigued and now wants to read it all. She commented that our adventure was one week before Sergeant Pepper was released. I have had no contact with Jim; we must try to trace him. There's a lot of catching up to do and we must find time this Autumn to do it. I must look out the legendary cine film and see if we can further look at what we did all those years ago. Thanks again for the log. I intend to reread more closely this week."

Jim and Dave back together again

October 16th 2013

Dave and Jim made arrangements to meet for their reunion at the Oaken Arms in Codsall near Wolverhampton, a venue roughly half-way between them. Jim was concerned they might not recognise each other after so many years. He joked that perhaps, like the spies of the Cold War, they should wear a red carnation and carry a copy of The Times newspaper. Dave thought this a brilliant idea and did just that. What an emotional reunion; they laughed and hugged each other, brilliant. Would their first words be as epic as Stanley's "Dr Livingstone I presume?" Jim's words were equally questioning: "Where's the loo?" he asked.

Dave and Jim enjoyed a splendid lunch and had a three-hour catch-up conversation. Every time Jim mentioned colleagues, Saltley and their P.E. experience, Dave produced memorabilia he had brought with him to illustrate their experiences. All too soon the meeting came to an end, but not before their waiter used Dave's camera to take a photo of them at their table. Dave and Jim promised to keep in contact. Jim said he would try to find his colour slides of their canoe adventure. They hoped Rog would still have his cine film record of it.

Post-Saltley Reunions

Dave and Roger reunite after 40 years

November 6th 2013

Rog informed Dave that he and Linda had booked a cottage in Church Stretton, Shropshire for a week's holiday in early November. It would be a good opportunity for them to meet and reminisce after more than 40 years.

Dave and Rog arranged to meet, with their wives, at the restaurant at the Ludlow Food Centre at 12.00pm on 6th November. It was equally as emotional as the meeting Dave had with Jim. Many hugs later you would never have guessed that over 40 years separated their last meeting. Dave had brought with him the memorabilia of the Saltley years that had impressed Jim. Linda vividly remembered receiving a phone call in April 1967 from Rog telling her he was near the end of the expedition and he would be at Kidderminster later that night. She related that Rog, ever the romantic, asked if there was any chance she could meet him at the canal in Kidderminster. He did apparently have the courtesy to warn her that he hadn't shaved for 12 days: but washing and a change of clothes was not mentioned. Undeterred, or perhaps because love is blind, she gathered two of her closest friends and went

to meet him and his two fellow canoeing friends. Her passion at meeting with Rog was immediate, it was a magic moment in their lives; but Dave was quick to say: "Enough of that! Give us a lift to get these canoes out of the water".

They could have talked for hours but the waiters were anxious to clear the tables. Rog said he would try to find his cine films of Saltley and see if they could be transferred to DVD.

In January 2014 Jim informed Dave he had located his colour slides and most of them were sound. Soon after, Rog let it be known he had ventured into his loft and found his old cine films. He was investigating companies that could transfer

All together again, after so many years

them onto a DVD. During February, Dave received copies of Jim's photos and at the end of the month Rog was excited to announce the successful transfer of his films onto disc. He hoped the three families could get together for a preview and suggested booking a long weekend from 4th-7th April at Monkhall Cottages near Hereford. Dave agreed but Jim had commitments and could only come on the Saturday when he and Margaret were collecting Beth from Bristol University.

The screening of the 25-minute "Saltley College 1964-67" DVD was spellbinding for the memories invoked. In three parts, the film recorded their 1966 P.E. Field Course in Snowdonia, the 1967 Wye/Severn canoeing adventure, and athletics on the college field. Rog presented Dave and Jim with copies for them to keep. Dave shared a letter from his son Nigel who suggested the log should be developed into a book to mark the adventure's 50th anniversary. Rog and Jim agreed and accepted Dave's offer to edit their log.

Plans were made to meet again in 12 months' time. Tintern, Chepstow and the Estuary would be essential to visit next time. Perhaps their old P.E. tutor Steve Allatt could be contacted to see if he remembered them and their expedition?

Dave contacted John Hyslop, secretary of the Old Salts Association (Steve had been a previous secretary) and asked if he had Steve's current contact details. He had and forwarded them. Dave immediately sent an email to Steve and asked if he could recall him and his canoeing adventure with Jim and Rog.

On 21st June 2014, Steve replied: "What a pleasure to hear from you after all these years and to be able to catch up on news of Roger and Jim. Firstly, and to gladden your hearts, not only was your expedition 'A magnificent achievement,' but was also the most outstanding of all those it was my pleasure to supervise. Having stressed that I would wish to add that there were many ventures of which participants could be justly proud and hopefully still give joy in recollection to those involved. As for 'Health and Safety' with your expedition – just don't go there! If there are other details which you feel might prove of assistance please do not hesitate to get back in touch. I hope you will appreciate that at 83 the powers of recall are not what they were. Meanwhile keep up the excellent work writing up your log and please pass on my best wishes to Roger and Jim. Kind regards, Steve."

Ed: In January 2016 came the sad news of Steve Allatt's passing. I was at his funeral. "R.I.P. Steve Allatt. 13.12.30 – 21.1.16."

Post-Saltley Reunions

17th – 20ᵗʰ April 2015

Dave and Rog again booked the Granary at Monkhall Cottages. Jim confirmed by email that he and Margaret would meet them in Chepstow on Sunday at 11.00am on the car park by the Information Centre near their original campsite on the banks of the Wye. They were all on time and quickly walked to where the men believed they had camped in 1967. But all was now very different.

The boatyard had gone and been replaced by concrete, tarmac and river embankments. Thankfully, they had brought their log and photos from 1967 and could orientate where they had made camp. They looked for the Lord Nelson pub only to discover that it was now a private dwelling. (There was a plaque on its wall that said it had previously been a public house and closed in 1966. They knew this was incorrect as they had supped there in April 1967.)

They then motored to Beachley and parked by the SARA (Severn Area Rescue Association) lifeboat station below the Severn Bridge. They gazed at the wide expanse of the estuary and the fast-flowing waters. Dave's wife Lynn said: "How stupid must you have been to canoe across that!" Margaret Murton and Linda Annable were equally incredulous. (If only they could have understood the blind ignorance their husbands had shown when venturing into the estuary in 1967.)

They made the short walk to the confluence of the Wye and Severn. Due to low water the exposed banks of the Wye were littered with debris and driftwood brought downriver. Margaret and Jim, as artists and recyclers, were in their element; they could see the potential of rescuing their finds and transforming them into works of art. They gathered a few choice bits but Margaret admonished Jim for being reluctant to

take hers to their car first. (Rog silently selected what he wanted and walked away.)

Eventually domestic harmony was restored. Next they all travelled 10 miles back up the Wye to where the men had camped opposite Tintern Abbey in 1967.

The wives viewed the ancient monument and then joined Dave, Rog and Jim for refreshments in the Anchor Inn. They persuaded a young girl from a nearby table to take a photo of them.

They returned to the Granary. After an excellent day they all agreed to meet in Gloucester the next year. Dave hoped to finish redrafting the Log by then and be able to give Rog and

Post-Saltley Reunions

It's changed a bit!

Jim a copy for their final approval and edit.

In April 2016 there was a day visit to Gloucester Docks. The area was very much changed from 1967. But it was nostalgic to see vessels moored nearby that they had seen all those years ago doing their work on the canal and in the estuary.

Dave gave Jim and Rog copies of the updated Log. They promised to evaluate it; and said they liked the cartoons. All was looking promising for completion of the written account of their adventure; but ill health halted Dave's progress.

In January 2017, with his health restored, Dave was able to revisit the Log and plan for the 50th Anniversary of the epic adventure.

The 50th Anniversary Reunion

Jim emailed Dave and Roger in February 2017 to say that April would be the 50th Anniversary of their epic canoe adventure. He suggested that, with Dave and Rog's approval, he should approach SARA (the Severn Area Rescue Association) to see if it would be possible for them to take the trio out onto the Severn Estuary in one of their inflatable lifeboat ribs. What better way to celebrate the 50th Anniversary? Approval was given and, following successful discussions with SARA (whose lifeboat station is located at Beachley on the west bank of the Severn, in the shadow of the first Severn Bridge), 27th April was confirmed as the date for the event.

The Three Men, back together again beside the River Wye

Thursday 27th April 2017, 6.45pm

Mervyn Fleming, Commander of SARA West Beachley Lifeboat & Rescue Station, greeted Dave, Jim and Rog on SARA's car park. He said that his team at Beachley were pleased to be able to provide an 'anniversary trip' down memory lane. Hopefully the experience would enable the trio to capture souvenir photos to complete the last pages of their Log. "Your expedition was unique at its time," said Mervyn, "and probably remains so."

A brief tour of the control centre, and introductions to the volunteer staff who operate it, was followed by Dave, Jim and Roger being kitted out in full safety waterproofs, helmets and lifejackets. They were now ready to be taken aboard the lifeboat rib 'James Hewitt'.

When the party was safely aboard, the rib was manoeuvred down the ramp and onto the estuary. The next hour surpassed their wildest expectations. They were taken at speeds up to 40 knots down to the second Severn Bridge, back upriver to the confluence of the Wye and the Severn, up to Chepstow, further upriver to Wintours Leap, before turning back to the Severn Estuary. And then Dave, Jim and Roger were each given control of the rib for a further exhilarating experience. When finally they stepped ashore, they were as elated as they'd been fifty years earlier.

A further surprise awaited the adventurers: James Hewitt, founder of SARA and the person after whom the rib in which they'd just travelled was named, was there to greet them. He explained that SARA had developed out of all recognition over the years, that the kernel of its formation was a result of discussions between a local doctor, with whom he sailed,

The 50th Anniversary Reunion

Arrival at SARA

Inside the Control Centre

and Captain William Groves – owner of the 'Firefly' whom the trio had met fifty years earlier, and one of the ferry engineers with whom he also sailed. Being the youngest of the four, James Hewitt ended up pushing the idea forward after the RNLI declined to fund a station at Beachley. He got the coastguard interested and, following a few casualties in the area, they agreed to form a Rescue Company comprising the original SARA members. He is now the sole survivor of this group.

Dave, Jim and Roger departed the Estuary with mixed emotions. They'd relived their estuary crossing from fifty years earlier but were aware that the adventure was now complete. They paused and thanked Saltley College, the Wye, Severn, two canoes and the Severn Area Rescue Association, for the adventures – and friendships – of a lifetime.

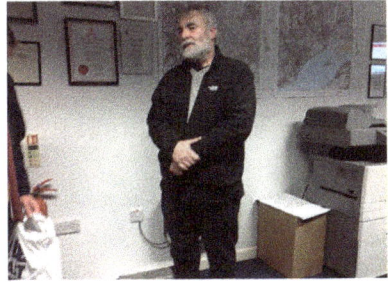

SARA Founder James Hewitt

Commander Fleming

Fearlessly embracing another adventure

About the Three Men

Roger Annable

Early Years

I remember being in a lecture with a group of 19-year-old prospective teachers and Physical Education students at Saltley College. The tutor was leading the session based on a book called 'Moving & Growing'. He talked about young boys running in the fields and 'brook jumping'. Whilst everyone was vaguely amused it didn't take long for me to realise that I'd pretty much had a 'textbook childhood'. Growing up in the 1950s in an East Midlands rural location I was always out in the open, completely free to climb trees, build dams and play all kind of games with a group of friends of similar age. We actually jumped into and over the local small river from Derbyshire into Nottinghamshire.

My home was in typical D.H. Lawrence country with woods, farms, coal mines, canals, railways and lakes on large estates. It was post war with 'rationing' still in existence; so you ate fresh vegetables from the garden and every scrap of food which mother expertly cooked and put on the table. There was not much money so nothing was wasted. There were a lot of us 'baby boomers' but we were very active, fit, healthy little boys. There were never enough hours in the day but we always came back home when 'called in' for Tea. We ran everywhere and became strong with bags of energy and stamina. Within a stone's throw there was a disused railway line on which coal had been transported to the 'Cut', an extension of the Grand Union Canal. The main Railway line from London to Scotland ran parallel to the canal with the small meandering river Erewash in between. We were always 'down the line' or in the wood and fields vaulting gates, jumping from heights, lighting camp-fires and having battles or swordfights with elder sticks which always ended with someone getting rapped on the fingers. Penknives were used to carve sticks or hit targets. Whether alone or in small groups, for us 'the Line' was a magnet for exploration and adventure.

All kind of risks were taken with no serious mishaps. Parents knew generally where you were and were happy to allow the freedom they had when they were young. You developed a lot of confidence to face up to scary things. Trying to get the 'shed number' on the boiler of engines, I can never forget the thrill of standing on a metal footbridge directly over the line as the Thames–Clyde express thundered towards me at 60 miles an hour passing feet below me and clouding me in smoke and steam. I was interested in everything; fishing in local ponds, running, chasing, climbing, balancing and challenging myself. To earn pocket money I dug and set vegetable gardens with my father and helped the milkman deliver milk and even drive the horse and cart. I always had a bike, which I had built, to cycle everywhere. My grandfather had owned a bike shop in the 1920s, my dad cycled to and from the knitwear factory every day so I knew everything about frames, paint spraying, gears, fixed wheels, handlebars, dynamos, brakes, spokes, tyres and how to mend punctures. I became very proficient at handling all kind of bikes at huge speeds and off- road.

I went alone to school on the trolley bus from the age of 5. When busses with engines took over I always leapt off the bus as it slowed for my stop and raced ahead of it into our gate.

The book 'Moving & Growing' followed youngsters at play which then developed into games, competitions and later formal sports; and so it was for me. We played football and cricket in the wood using two trees as goal posts or wickets. We kicked a tennis ball in the school yard and later on the pavement at home when the streetlights came on. It was short trousers every day until second year at Grammar School when team games became a real focus. We formed our own local youth teams and got some support from a few adults who officiated and coached us but we were largely self- taught. I was an all- rounder, pretty good at most things and practised constantly. With football, cricket, tennis, swimming, badminton, table tennis, golf, fishing, cycling and, of course, marbles we were never bored. There was no TV at home for most of us, not even telephones let alone mobile phones.

At the age of fourteen I began turning out for local adult teams who were short of players. As the only youngster in the team I was put on the right wing for Woodside Colliery Sports in the Notts. League and learned valuable lessons from the hard-working miners who forged an excellent spirit and looked after everyone in the team just like they looked after each other underground. "Football is a simple game," I was told, "stay wide, get past the full-back, behind their defence and centre the ball so our ex-Youth International Centre Forward can knock it in the net. Once you get past the full-back (probably in his late 30s) don't mess around and try to beat him a second time." That was good advice because if you did anything fancy it would make him look weak and he would kick you up in the air next time you got the ball. Yes, you learned to respect others in your team, your opponents and the weather conditions. We played in rain, snow, fog, bitterly cold wind and enjoyed playing in the mud getting absolutely plastered.

I sometimes struggled with the heavy leather ball which 'brained you' when you headed it and printed 'lace marks' on your forehead. It was all worth it afterwards with a steaming hot mug of tea in the piping hot Pithead Baths with the miners. We grew up quickly.

In the Summer it was cricket and I spent most days with the boys at Shipley Hall Cricket Club. I mowed the outfield, raked the square and batted in the nets. Several uncles were cricketers so I inherited their whites, which Mum altered. They enlisted me to score the games (I got half a crown and a free tea) which enabled me to study tactics, performances and eventually I played in the Senior team when they were short of players. At Shipley we had a Youth Team and my quick reactions served me well in developing as wicketkeeper. I wanted to be involved with every ball, concentrating intensely, anticipating what might happen and taking pride in stopping every ball. Standing up to the wicket you needed to look after yourself in a dangerous position and similarly when batting I was happy to face fast bowling. Graduating to Senior second then first teams, I came up against my uncles and some really good players. An early claim to fame as a 15-year-old was facing Bill Voce and hitting him for four. Yes, that's the 'Voce 'of 'Larwood & Voce' legendary England fast bowlers in the Bodyline Ashes series when we beat Australia. Mind you he was at the end of his career and bowling much slower. Cricket became my main sport. It was a team game but when you were batting it was one against eleven players on the other side…they were all trying to get you out. I identified Concentration and Determination as key factors I should keep on developing.

My decision to apply to Saltley was due to my Church of England background. My family was very involved with our local church; it was their social life. I was in the choir from about six years of age and regularly attended three services every Sunday. The clash with cricket on a Sunday led to a break in the frequency of attendance. (But I was still involved enough for the vicar to give me a glowing reference when I was recommended to apply to Saltley College.) Once at Saltley the break became permanent – I'd had a surfeit of religion.

At Saltley I played football in the first year. Probably 2/3rds. I fell out with the club in the second year and didn't play at all. I captained the 3rd's in my third year and enjoyed a very successful season. Also enjoyable was supporting the athletics team and officiating the field events on home matches.

1966/67 Football 3rd team. Roger is centre front, holding the ball.

How do you get into a situation where you start canoeing down one of our great rivers in the River Wye, intending to go more than 100 miles, then tackle some of the most difficult tidal waters of the Severn Estuary before another 80+ miles upstream via canals and the River Severn to Kidderminster? And at the start of the expedition knowing nothing of the inherent dangers and never having set foot in a canoe before? Well the short answer is that I thought the others were experts (Dave and Jim had already made a successful canoe expedition the previous year) and I liked a challenge.

Dave and Jim had come up with the idea of this fantastic journey and they had an outline organisation to achieve it. I came late to their project. College had canoes I could borrow and tag along…simple. The three of us got on well, had done so much together for three years and lived in adjacent Middle South rooms at Saltley. As part of our Physical Education course we had done climbing, abseiling and camping in North Wales, sometimes in dreadful conditions. Ironically, the programmed canoeing on that course had been cancelled due to poor weather. My 8mm cine camera had captured our exploits on that course, so adding an extra canoe into their plans but being able to film their expedition had to be a good deal. I was confident that Dave and Jim had the experience behind them to help me, especially with crossing the Estuary, which my research noted, was a dangerous area even for experienced canoeists in the calmest of conditions. I was elated when they agreed to me joining them on what was now our expedition of 'three men in two canoes'.

I anticipated bacon and egg for breakfast; Dave and Jim could not believe I had never experienced sausage and egg. No packed lunches; from what I remember we existed after breakfast on biscuits and chocolate and fags during the day. For our evening meal, tinned Fray Bentos stewed steak and baked beans were staples. We ate lots of white sliced bread and jam and drank instant coffee; the water boiled in billy cans on the primus stove. What joy to have the occasional fish and chips on our travels. Did we eat well? Probably not.

On reflection it was all very naïve. We believed we were invincible and would succeed. Our culture at Saltley convinced us that we "Salts" were the best and could achieve anything we set our minds to; often against the odds. We had faith we could develop our canoeing skills and techniques as we went along. Over the first week I could even practise going aground and capsizing. All three of us were confident we could meet the daily challenges and encourage each other on our canoeing adventure. The inescapable fact that I had not canoed before never crossed my mind. I never considered for one moment that my inexperience in a canoe could endanger our lives or the success of our adventure.

Post-Saltley Experiences

After the Expedition, we all successfully completed the teacher training course to qualify and take up posts as specialist teachers of physical education. My first post was in charge of Physical Education in Coventry's State Boarding School in South Shropshire not far from Ludlow and Bridgnorth. Basketball, rugby, athletics and cross country teams excelled at the school. I found time also to build my own marine-ply racing canoe and spent many weekends taking half a dozen youngsters canoe camping on the River Teme. The School Trailer dropped us off on Friday evening and picked up Sunday afternoon with no one questioning why there was only one adult supervising the group, miles from anywhere.

I married Linda in London in 1968 (she had greeted us at the end of the Expedition) and lived in a 'married flat' taking responsibility for the Annex, a dormitory for 30 boys. I played football and cricket for Cleobury Mortimer and Linda taught in the Town Primary School. After three years we followed former colleagues from the City of Coventry School to the Bahama Islands. Here was another big challenge on the other side of the world; living by the sea on an island in a settlement of 1,000 people (we were the only white people).

We signed a three-year contract with the Ministry of Overseas Development who were helping the Government of the Bahamas to rapidly raise the standard of their education prior to Independence. We set about teaching, also teaching the teachers how to teach, and developing sport on the island. We built a Sports Association with Directors of Sports and ran regular sporting competitions between schools in the various towns. An annual athletics sports was the highlight, with an 8-lane track drawn and personally marked out in creosote at the airport. Judges stood on Aircraft steps and there was even a Steeplechase with a water jump through the lake by the runway. We had no hot water, TV; read many books often by candlelight and for periods of time acted as Postmaster and Headteacher. We were well respected by parents of the 300 pupils in the school and returned to England reflecting on a trip into the unknown, where determination had been called upon to complete what we had set out to do, in testing circumstances.

In Whitstable I took the best job on offer in the U.K. at the time: heading up a big P.E. Department in a 1,000+ Secondary School. Featuring in the management of the school made for a demanding life.

There were many innovations, including devising an Examination in Physical Education with, of course, an outdoor pursuits & camping field-course using the nearby Nonington College. After 24 years I was Head of P.E., Senior Teacher, Director of 6th Form Studies, Teacher Governor, School Business & Lettings Manager, i/c minibuses and heading for a heart attack or burn-out. The school was getting smaller and had to incentivise the reduction of teacher numbers thus providing a unique opportunity for me to take

Early Retirement & Redundancy. Financially this was made possible since Linda was continuing to teach in the local Swalecliffe Primary School.

However, a year later, I was urgently recalled to the school by the Head teacher. He asked me to spearhead Business & Letting, Adult Learning and set up the first Online Learning Centre (Learndirect). I sat on the Kent Board of Learndirect for many years.

During the late '70s, '80s, and '90s, alongside teaching we found time to bring up a family and do a host of other interesting things. We are lucky to have a son and daughter who both attended University and gained good Law Degrees. Victoria went on to complete a glittering career in PR, Advertising & Events Management in London. She now lives locally, runs Whitstable Literary Festival and has two delightful young boys Luke and Duncan. They love being outside and eagerly follow 'Grandpa' outdoors in the garden and on the beach. Ross is a legal manager in a big French Construction, Property, International Business in London. He is well travelled and has good links also with USA where he studied American Law at the University of Texas. As a teenager he played County Cricket for Kent and his young son Rory ensures the Annable name will continue. My sporting career continued as long as possible, playing soccer for University of Kent Staff in the Canterbury league until carried off the field with a cartilage injury. Cricket continued to a high standard as a wicketkeeper/batsman for Chestfield C.C. often playing all-day games against County and International teams. Somehow I also included setting up a very successful Colts Section at the Club and chairing it for 20 years as well as sitting on the main club executive management committee.

Early retirement enabled me to develop my interest in

forging twinning links with towns in Europe. The Whitstable Twinning Association (WTA) I'd set up for Whitstable in 1987, initially with one German Partnertown grew to take in five more in France, Denmark, Sweden, East Germany and Czech Republic, then eventually five more friendship links with more than 1,000 people travelling annually to and from Whitstable. The traditional twinning model was torn up and replaced to establish 'People in Partnership' on modern independent, self-financing, cutting-edge lines. I had travelled widely in USA, Canada, West Indies and Mexico during the time in the Bahamas. Family holidays with a young family in Whitstable involved annually towing a caravan in France. WTA offered a possibility for ordinary people to visit friends in Partnertowns in Europe & beyond with travel & everything organised for them. Whitstable is only a half hour drive to Dover and nowadays the Channel Tunnel gets you in France in a further half hour. Sports teams, Clubs and Organisations across Whitstable could add an International Dimension to their activities. I took sports teams abroad and Sixth Form Students made exchange visits every year with me for 15 years as part of their European Studies. High profile biennial International Teacher Conferences and Teacher Exchanges were developed. It was a huge privilege to represent Whitstable on the International stage and very good firm friends have been made throughout this unique interlinked Network of Partnertowns in and beyond Europe. It pushed me to speak French and German languages almost fluently. Whitstable/Borken was recognised as the Number One Anglo /German twinning link and the WTA probably the best UK independent association. After Chairing Whitstable Twinning Association for 30 hugely successful years, I passed the baton to younger people and took on its Presidency.

They say "If you want something done, then give it to a busy person!" Twice I turned down requests to revitalise Whitstable Castle, an 18th Century Manor House given to the Town for Community purposes. However, I relented and in 2003 took on the project as Castle Co-ordinator to run it for the next five years. Getting approved wedding venue status, among various initiatives, turned around the fortunes of the Castle and eventually it proved attractive enough to be awarded a five million pound Heritage Lottery Grant for complete restoration of the Castle and Grounds. Since 2005 I have also promoted a local young very talented Performing Arts Company which began at the Castle. 'Phoenix Performing Arts' specialises in Dance and Musical Theatre and I assisted them to get a grant of £50,000 to get a permanent studio. Honoured as Patron, I continue helping to take youngsters abroad, as feedback shows that it helps build confidence and independence in those late teenage/early20ís impressionable years. In 2014, using my International contacts, I organised for 35 young actors from the PPA to perform Shakespeare's Romeo and Juliet in a two week tour to Sweden & Denmark promenading in castles and churches. The reviews were glowing and for those youngsters it was unforgettable.

In August 2018 Linda and I celebrated our Golden Wedding Anniversary. We had met for the first time at a Big Beat Night at Saltley College 23rd October 1965. The band were the Mighty Avengers, Decca recording stars, who had just released their record of 'So Much In Love With You' written by Jagger and Richards of the Rolling Stones. It charted in the top fifty that week.

One can regularly pose the sometimes unanswerable question "What if" at many incidents, decisions, or the crossroads of life. How would things have been? Everyone can pose these questions and get different answers. I can say that my time as a student at Saltley was highly significant. The friendships we made, the quality of our teaching training and our sporting opportunities shaped our future lives. On reflection, the canoeing expedition and especially the crossing of the Severn Estuary was a bigger success than we thought at the time. We did not know that no one had previously completed the total course of our 180 miles. Now fifty years later we believe our adventure has not been replicated. Yes it was foolhardy, dangerous and poorly planned but we made it.

This book is a testament to what we achieved and proof of a unique adventure.

Roger with cine camera, Snowdon 1966

Roger 'Jim' Murton

Early Years

I had never thought about becoming a schoolteacher until I was about sixteen. I'd always been interested in sport but my main passion was aviation. I had built model aircraft from the age of five and dreamed of joining the RAF. However, my academic qualifications meant I had no chance of becoming a pilot or senior aircrew. I had a talent for design and considered architecture for a career.

Then my maths and games teacher at school suggested to my father that I should consider P.E. teaching. (This teacher used to play for Queens Park Rangers but, as an avid supporter of Derby County, I have never held this against him.)

That was it, decision made. I gained the exam results required and undertook student unqualified teaching in a local school for twelve months prior to gaining a place at college. This teaching experience reinforced my belief I was making the right choice of career.

What college to apply for? Without professional guidance and not fully knowing what I was doing, I applied first choice to Loughborough. (Silly me – they didn't even grant me an interview.) By chance I met a male friend of my sister who had qualified at Saltley. He said what a great place it was. I applied and, as you know, the rest is history.

Details about life at college are extensive and difficult to list. However, I do remember feeling how close and friendly the place was; not just close friends or the P.E. group but the whole place. It was a real community.

The first thing for me to say about Saltley was how well it equipped us for teaching. Every activity we undertook, whether in the gym, on the games field, in the swimming pool or elsewhere was geared to how we might teach children – invaluable. I remember taking my prepared primary lesson in the gym (my P.E. colleagues were the class) and uttering the classic line: "And what else can you do with your bean bags?" The proffered suggestions would have been very painful to carry out. How about the country dancing practised there? Those swords, which were meant to interlink so that one of us could hold the lot above his head, oh dear. And those modern dance classes at Anstey College, with their female students and their camp male dance tutor, remain memorable. While my colleagues posed like trees in the wind, I was determined to give this new experience my all. After one very strenuous session, I was approached by the tutor who tapped me on the shoulder. I expected him to praise my athleticism and dedication, but I was stunned by his comment: "Nice arse Mr. Murton".

I vividly remember my first night at college. On arrival there was a third year student in the Porter's Lodge who helped me with my trunk – yes my trunk – to my room in Middle South. When he left, I looked around the room. It had gloss green paintwork with dark oak furniture. It was basic, like a monk's cell in a monastery. There was worse to come as I opened the metal-framed window and looked out. Below me was the Morris Commercial factory. I looked down through the roof lights and could see the workers on the night shift. There was a nauseous smell of cellulose and I thought, "What have I done?" However, after a few days, I realised that

Saltley College was a great place. Perhaps we took the original old buildings for granted but we came to realise they were beautiful and unique. South block even smelt clean; the cleaners took a pride in their work and looked after us well.

How about the meals in the first year? The formal sit-down evening meals beginning with grace being spoken by a member of the Student Council from the top table. (Sadly in future years, meals were less formal, being collected cafeteria style.) The oak-panelled main dining room was stunning. Who can forget the cream buns and cakes mid-afternoon? Did anyone check if we queued more than once? The other food memories must, of course, include the pub across the road from the gym. We really enjoyed those Friday lunches at The Country Girl, before taking a lecture and swimming lesson with Blackjack – also known as Bill Middleton.

The traditions were memorable; like the leek-eating competition. This was a time to appreciate not being Welsh. It was painful seeing our passionate colleagues from the Valleys devouring the vegetable at speed and then spewing it back up. Perhaps the most memorable, however, was the Saltley Rocket at Christmas end of term. All of us shuffling silently together through the college into the quad and circling the Holy Acre. There for the Senior Student to walk onto the sacred grass and light an imaginary rocket. The silence then broken by 300 students shouting "WHOOSH!" What an atmosphere; in all of my three years, the silence and tradition of the Link was honoured. And I can't remember anybody during those years taking a short cut across the grass in the quad.

When we arrived at college in September 1964 we were given a description of the College Traditions written by Major Osborne. I still have my copy and so can accurately quote what he wrote:

"College Traditions." We are fortunate in having at St. Peter's a quadrangle which is the obvious centre of the College. We are also fortunate in having a history which we can be proud of, and throughout the life of the College there have been occasions where all members have met in the quadrangle to express their brotherhood. Recently an Old Salt who was here in the 1880s came to College, escorted by an elderly grand-daughter, stood in the quad and described the ceremonies he shared in with great detail: he even recited the names of the men in his year in alphabetical order.

It is impossible to say how old these ceremonies are, except that "The Link" was practised in the 1860s. In the 1880s there were two occasions when the quadrangle was used, the first on Recruits' Night when the new year was enrolled in the College Company of Volunteers. This occurred near the beginning of the first term and consisted of a meeting in the Dining Hall followed by an assembly in the quadrangle. In those days there was a lamp standard in the centre of the green, and on these occasions only the lamp was lit and the Senior Student stood under it, traditionally he is the only man in the College allowed to stand on this grass. On Recruits' Night meeting, which was still being held in the 1920s, the National Anthem was sung.

The other ceremony, "The Link", takes place at the end of the Michaelmas Term because in the early days the academic year began in January and ended in September. Then, as now, men came from all parts of the country and from overseas. When they came they found College life to be very hard and the routine severe. There were few occasions in term time when men were allowed leave from College, and students had to live an isolated and cloistered life. This had its advantages in that men were thrown together far more and there was far more sharing of joys and sorrows. This built up a truly remarkable communion of spirit, and the bond of affection symbolised in "The Link" was a true one. We still like to think of the members of St. Peter's College are still "linked" both in College and afterwards.

Roger 'Jim' Murton

For the benefit of new members of the College it is perhaps necessary to describe the form of the ceremony, and this is the modern pattern, which is in all essentials the same as the ancient form.

The whole student body assembles in line on the college field with the buildings completely in darkness. The Senior Student takes his place at the head of the column and each man places his hands on the shoulders of the man in front. The College then proceeds, very slowly and in complete silence through the cloisters by the side of the Hall, along the corridor round the south and east sides of the quadrangle, into the quadrangle, then circles slowly until all the men are moving in concentric circles round the green. All members then stop and face inwards and the Senior Student takes up his place on the green. The College then sings in order one verse from "The First Nowell", "Hark the Herald Angels Sing", "Home Sweet Home". This is followed by the Saltley Rocket, after which the college disperses in silence. When the quadrangle is clear, and not before, the lights go on once again and the ceremony is over. From the beginning to the end of the ceremony there should be no talking of any sort. During the whole time, and especially during the singing you should think of your fellows and of the men who have gone before and therefore perpetuate "The Link".

It is a simple but most impressive ceremony, and properly performed exerts a real binding force. Especially in the old days this was the occasion when men were accepted as part of the brotherhood of Salts, and the link is intended to express the genuine affection for each other which we hope is still a feature of the community life of Saltley.

Major Osborne

[Taken from The Guide to Saltley, *published by* The Students Union of St. Peter's College, Saltley *which was presented to new students in September 1964.]*

1965/66 Football 2nd Team. Jim is on the back row, second from the right.

What Saltley student could ever forget Teaching Practice with the famous red books in which we recorded our lesson plans and schemes? The joy of returning to college at the end of each day and seeing that someone had already chalked on the Porter's notice board how many days were left of the practice.

I loved athletics on the college field and the unique challenge of running around a 330-yard egg shaped grass track. Memorable was the time when I was competing against an international sprinter from Birchfield Harriers in the 220-yards. He took off like a Formula 1 racing car and left me for dead. Unfortunately he failed to negotiate the tight left bend and departed the track crashing into the netting of the tennis courts. I swept past and have always enjoyed (albeit by default) the bragging rights of my victory. I regularly competed in the Long Jump and also what was then called the Hop, Skip and Jump. (I was thrilled to be awarded my Athletics Colours in 1967. In football I had been a regular of the second XI for three years, but colours were only awarded to outstanding first team players.)

I regularly finished my jumps face down in the landing pit; there to pound the sand in disgust and frustration. I am often reminded that if sand throwing became an Olympic event, then I was your man.

In my final football match for my school team, I went up for a corner, tried to head the ball but instead headed my own player's head. He sustained a minor cut but I lost two front teeth. I was on a football refresher course when the coach asked me to pass the ball to a colleague. I did it very badly. The coach's reprimand was terse: "Where I come from we have a collection for people like you."

Cricket also had its moments. I was about to bowl my first ball when the 'keeper turned to first slip and asked "What does Murton bowl?" The reply has always hurt: "There's no point asking me. He doesn't know himself!"

What experiences did I bring to our canoe expedition? Camping was not new to me. I had previously been climbing and walking in the Lake District, North Wales and on the Isle of Skye. However, the new bit was water. Water had always fascinated me though, especially when I stayed with relatives in Bournemouth. I was spoilt there with the sea and rivers. This was the time I made model boats. Any type of craft on water fascinated me. I even used to watch TV shows/films where the native American used their birch bark canoes to travel to really inaccessible places because of their shallow draught and light weight. I used to dream of how exciting it would be to explore an unknown river. Little did I know that I would have such an opportunity on our expedition. There is only one thing that could have made our trip even more special: I would love to have made the canoes myself.

Post-Saltley Experiences

I started my teaching career at Belper Pottery secondary school in Derbyshire (1967-1970). This was a small secondary modern school with very poor facilities for physical education, but it certainly encouraged me to improvise. Most lessons were taken outdoors – weather permitting. These were on the school playground. To work inside meant removing desks and chairs, stacking them outside under an overhanging roof. An extra challenge was that the P.E. store was across the playground. The indoor area was also a classroom and the school hall. The games field was also the local recreation ground about two hundred metres from the main buildings. Swimming took place in the local baths, a typical late Victorian building with a balcony and green and white tiles. The elderly couple that managed it had normally just finished breakfast when we arrived, so the aroma was a mixture of chlorine and food cooked in fat which had clearly been used more than once. Not put off, I used to return one evening a week to take evening classes which involved examining for personal survival qualifications.

I inherited the position of cross-country secretary. This was often quite entertaining, as the county championships were sometimes in wintry conditions. It was Derbyshire after all. Ice skating became a regular after school activity. I was encouraged by our art teacher, who had for some years been learning 'ice dance'. She was only too willing to join us and coach the children (and me). Like most schools, outdoor pursuits were part of the P.E. programme. We had an excellent centre nearby and made annual visits. A trip abroad – to Switzerland – was enjoyed in my time there. The accompanying staff enjoyed it so much that we went to Spain the following year – but without the pupils! There was also a Youth Club, attached to the school, which was attended by many ex-pupils. The Head teacher (who regularly attended) persuaded me with the help of some of the older club members to enter their football team into a local league.

After three years I moved to Ashby Ivanhoe high school. It was part of the Leicestershire plan with pupils between the ages of eleven and fourteen. It had a gymnasium! I taught at this school for seven very happy years during which, like all P.E. teachers, covered a full range of activities. However, I took a particular interest in athletics – having contact with clubs in Derby and Leicester. To help with winter training, I organised Sunday morning sessions at school. This was made easier with the support of the caretaker who would willingly open the school for me. When I thanked him, he used to say: "It's okay because it's for the children". A great guy. Friday afternoons for one year were a little different, as I was teaching the ROSLA (Raising of the School Leaving Age) pupils. I organised a programme that often involved use of the school minibus. It was always very reluctant to start. To answer this problem, the pupils pushed it around the playground until it 'bump started'. I don't remember any risk assessments being done in those days, or health and safety checks. Oops!

Besides working a full P.E. programme, I became Parents and Teachers Association (PTA) secretary, organising many events such as folk nights, wine tasting evenings and the summer fair. Once again we enjoyed a trip abroad, this time to Italy. The enthusiastic staff at this school also found time for the staff panto at Christmas.

From the Ivanhoe in Ashby-de-la-Zouch I moved on to Heathfield High School in Earl Shilton, again in Leicestershire. Here I took up the post of Head of year. I think my only claim to fame in this role was that in one academic year I had the largest intake of pupils in Leicestershire. We had 332 pupils join us that year, which meant the formation of 12 tutor groups (classes). I thought it was going to be difficult leaving the Ivanhoe, but in the end I remained at Heathfield until retirement. During this time, like many colleagues, I saw several major changes in schools, including the National Curriculum and SATs. It was also a time of 'new initiatives'. I was not too fond of some of those. Looking back I really enjoyed my teaching career. It was helped enormously by having such a good grounding at Saltley. I think we taught through the best of times. The schools were happy and teachers could be creative. We were trusted. How today's teachers cope with the constant pupil monitoring, testing and being monitored themselves I don't know.

During my time as a P.E. teacher (like many of my friends from college) I took part in sport myself, with football in the winter and cricket in the summer. I played football until my late twenties when I found that refereeing on a Saturday morning and playing in the afternoon was becoming a little tiring! I was always amused when I turned up for the afternoon game in my dirty boots from the morning, sitting next to team members from other professions with their very clean boots! Then my panic when the captain would say: "Let's go and warm up lads'. This was not at the forefront of my thoughts.

Outside of sport, I've always had a bit of a love/hate relationship with classic cars. However, being on a teacher's salary meant I was frequently financially embarrassed; my bank balance would have improved if I had avoided them. None of them were 'show' cars and needed regular repairs and 'tender loving care'. Also they were needed to get me to work every day in all weathers. They were not just brought out on sunny weekends. Here's the list of cars I owned: MG Midget, Lotus 7 series2 (Perhaps I was influenced by 'The Prisoner' TV programme?),

Triumph TR4, Riley RMA, VW Beetle Cabriolet, Land Rover 90, Gilbern Invader MK2, Saab 900 turbo. The Lotus had the petrol filler cap inside the car. In the days when attendants served you they looked on in amazement when I pulled up the hood and said: "In there please". The tank also slopped and leaked a little sometimes, so when returning exercise books to school (that I had marked the previous evening) I had to warn the class to 'not light a match!'

I did a long continental tour in the Riley one year. It meant carrying a full tool kit and grease gun, as the car needed a service every 1,000 miles. In one petrol station in Germany, the attendant asked about the age of the car. "Thirty five years," I replied. He looked at the car, then at his wife standing nearby and said, "My wife is the same, but I think your car is in better condition." I once had the VW Beetle repatriated from France after it badly overheated on a main road north of Paris. The RAC were great; the recovery man arrived and said he would have to transport the car to his garage on the back of his truck. It was a beautiful hot day and we had the hood down on the Beetle, so the recovery man suggested we would be more comfortable and cooler sitting in our car on the truck bed than riding in his cab. That was fine until his route took us through a village that was celebrating a carnival for 'The Cat and the Dog'. Suddenly we realised we looked like the last float in the parade. Everyone was waving and cheering us as we drove through. We joined in and had a great time.

After retiring from teaching, I realised that I could pursue an interest that I had craved all my life: being creative in designing and making bespoke furniture and contemporary pieces. I particularly enjoyed recycling abandoned materials into works of art. Working part time from home was perfect, as our daughter Beth had been born shortly before I left Heathfield.

This was excellent as it gave me more time to spend with her, especially when she was young. When Beth was at primary school I was asked to join the governing body of her school. I accepted but never thought I'd become Vice Chairman and remain so for ten years. It was a great experience seeing another side of school life; and I was with a dedicated and superb set of people voluntarily giving their expertise and time to enhance the educational opportunities of our children. How quickly the years fly by, as Beth is now training in Norwich Medical School to become a doctor.

My wife Margaret is a musician and also an artist, enabling us to combine our interests in a new chapter of our lives. We have both exhibited in galleries around the country and shops such as Liberty in London and David Hicks Interiors.

My own work has continued mostly through private commissions where people want individually crafted furniture for their houses. However, I have realised I have to stop such work when the pieces to be made are getting larger (and heavier) and I am getting physically weaker. From now on, I am returning to much smaller items and joining Margaret in some joint ventures. As a hobby, I have taken on the challenge of designing and building a small motorboat. What was I saying earlier about getting weaker? It seems that, where water's involved, one can summon the strength when required. Just as we did all those years ago.

It was a fabulous experience.
I don't think we realised the magnitude
of what we had achieved.

David Hudson

Early Days

I was born in 1944 at 64 Doversley Road, Birmingham. This was my home for the next nine years. There was a lamp post a few yards down the road. I spent hours playing around this and attempting to shin up it to its two arms. I remember the joy of reaching the top for the first time; though not without the necessary bunking and shoving from my brothers below. Later I managed to pull myself up, sit on the arms and cradle the lamp. From that moment I imagined I was king of the road; high and safe, on a par with my older brothers, but away from their poking and teasing. I guess I was about seven.

Games around the lamp, hopscotch on the slab pavement; I think we chalked and numbered eight slabs and skimmed a stone or piece of slate. Falling over usually brought further distress to already grazed and bruised knees; the penalty of wearing short trousers.

Marbles of glass with a shiny eye were keenly competed for; but they were light and easily despatched by a large ball bearing. Chips and breaks were frequent and in some of our games the heavy silver ball was banned.

Cricket was played in the street, with the lamp post as wicket. What arguments my brothers and I had while playing. Bowled, caught, run out – all to be disputed; but if the big boys said you were out, you were out. How I longed to be a big boy.

Cricket bats were cut from a plank; rough handles blistering and splintering tender hands. The balls, thankfully, were soft and rubbery and easily sent bouncing down the road by the big hitters. But they were not so easy for me to chase after and attempt to throw back up the sloping road. The shouts of "get a move on" rang out as I struggled to overtake the rolling ball. A quick hard throw and a direct hit would see the batsman run out. This was the intention but rarely the result. My aim was good but my arm weak. What laughter from other players as my puny efforts failed to reach halfway before rolling back to me. I became a good fielder of my own throws.

A meeting place in the evening and the base for hide and seek. "99, 100, ready or not here I come!" What plans we hatched for our amusement. The imagination and thrill of cowboys and Indians; bows, arrows, guns; all hand-made, crude, but to our fertile minds they were the real thing. The dramatic fall and collapse when shot. "Bang you're dead!" The cowboys always won, galloping away on their imaginary horses, slapping their thighs as they ran.

We had less social games: "Tap and run" – the knocking at a door and running off before it was answered. Giggling behind a wall as an irate neighbour appeared at their door. "Clear off you little buggers!" was hurled in our direction. We usually did – until the next time.

At the bottom of the road, behind some flats, was a canal; narrowboats pulled by horse, the occasional fisherman, but generally still and quiet water; a narrow channel between the reeds, black ash towpaths, a hawthorn hedge, myriad of pond life, but essentially an extended playground for us kids. Here we built and sailed real rafts. Four empty oil drums, planks and rope were all that was needed. There were always willing hands for the building but not many volunteered for being first on board.

Once a brave soul proved that the raft could float, everyone wanted a turn. We were pirates and adventurers; Tom Sawyer and Huck Finn running with the wind, having fun, undisturbed by adults.

Derek, my oldest brother, had a lovely wooden sledge; his pride and joy and the envy of others on the snowy slopes. It always seemed a shame that it hung, unused, in our garage for most of the year. It occurred to me, on one hot and sunny summer's day, that it would be a good idea to take the sledge to the canal to see if it would float. It floated well enough – until I put my foot on it. Quickly regaining my footing on the towpath, I watched in horror as the sledge resurfaced but out of reach. A gentle breeze began to move the sledge further out into midstream current and towards the opening of the "mile tunnel"; if it entered there all would be lost. Despite my frantic attempts to reach the sledge, throwing bricks and poking it with a stick, the sledge sailed on. The towpath ended at the tunnel mouth: I stood there helpless and desolate as my brother's pride and joy disappeared from sight. I knew only too well the trouble I could expect when my stupidity was discovered. With a resigned sigh and cursory muttering, I turned for home. The immediate retribution was nothing compared to the constant harping back to this incident at family gatherings ever since. Derek also reminds everyone that he would have been wealthy if I hadn't, on another occasion, melted down his collection of lead soldiers. I guess I was about eight.

Of my brothers and sisters, Derek, (born in 1935) was often charged with looking after me. I remember his piggy-backs but especially being carried sitting on his shoulders. He held my legs and I steered by pulling on his ears. Michael (born 1940) loved animals and birds. He reared an owl. Doing so was sufficiently unusual in those days for an article to appear about it in the Birmingham Evening Mail. A photograph was included: Michael with the owl and me alongside holding a tortoise. We looked a right pair of urchins. Bryan (born 1941) had an inquisitive and scientific mind. He was an expert at dismantling and repairing anything electrical. He would tinker for hours in the shed at the bottom of our garden. I recall the banger guns he made from copper pipe. The pipe would be fixed in a vice, one end sealed, gunpowder taken from fireworks rammed in, followed by nuts and nails, and ignited by match. The resulting bang was impressive but the damage to the shed wall (and the exploding pipe that just missed us) brought a halt to further experiments. Bryan also made a catapult from a forked twig and elastic gave enough power for him to fire a small stone. I was walking up the road towards him one day when he called out "Stop or I will fire!" I didn't, he did. The stone bounced once, reared up and hit me in the mouth. One of my new front teeth was snapped in half. I had a distinctive jagged tooth for the next six years until it was capped by a sympathetic dentist. I was born in 1944, followed in 1947 by twin sisters, Anne and Elizabeth. Sadly one died after three minutes and the other after three days. This I have been told but I have no memory of the trauma this must have caused my parents and brothers. The last of my siblings, Patricia, was born in 1953. Her arrival posed a potential accommodation problem for our small semi-detached and my parents looked for a larger property. We moved to Kinver, South Staffordshire, the day after my ninth birthday: 14th December 1953. Although only twenty miles away, the move brought to an abrupt end my friendships in Birmingham. I know I was sad.

I made good progress at Kinver Junior school and my parents hoped I might be the first of their sons to pass the 11+ exam for entry to a Grammar School. I messed up on the maths paper by not noticing there were questions on the back page. Consequently I did not complete enough for a pass mark. I did not experience the disappointment of failure: Grammar school would have meant Saturday morning lessons, wearing a school cap, learning French and Latin and playing rugby.

Kinver Secondary School gave me a happy environment; plenty of sport and responsibilities: Head Boy, Captain of football, cricket and athletic teams, Speaker for the prize-winning Young Farmers public speaking team, House and Form Captain; and top of the class in exams. But the teachers expected their students to be academic failures and not achieve a professional career. Thus we were guided towards manual and menial jobs. The curriculum featured gardening and woodwork for the boys, needlework and cooking for the girls. Basic English, maths, geography, history, art, music, rural science for the boys, biology for the girls; all leading to the award, if successful, of the Staffordshire Leaver's certificate. The headmaster started a fencing club and I learnt to fence with the foil. I was entered for and won the West Midlands Schools fencing championships in 1960. I then progressed to the National finals of the English Schools Championships held at Weston, Somerset: I reached the quarter-finals.

Although the school was planning a fifth form to offer the chance of doing "O" levels I opted to move to Halesowen College of Further Education to undertake a two year O-Level course from 1960-62. I achieved good pass grades in five subjects. Instead of progressing to "A" levels I accepted an offer from the headmaster at my old school to return as a student teacher and apply for teacher training.

I was called to interview at Alsager college to specialise in Physical Education. I had to undergo tests in physical ability and gymnastics and knew I had performed very successfully and better than the other applicants. However, the P.E. examiner informed me that I would not be accepted on the course as I was inappropriately dressed. His advice was: "Next time you go for interview make sure you have white shorts, vest and footwear when asked to show your ability." Obviously he found my bare chest, black shorts and pumps offensive. Why hadn't they included this advice in the invitations sent to applicants?

My next application to Loughborough was dismissed without a call to interview; my next interview at Dudley College went well until I was asked if I had any political or religious opinions. I was confused and replied that I had but didn't wish to discuss them. They must have judged me a dissident and troublemaker; a letter informed me that I was unsuccessful in my application. No other college offered me an interview, so I stayed teaching unqualified at Kinver for another year.

In late October 1963 I applied to join the Police Force and was called to interview in Birmingham. I matched all the requirements for academic standards and matched the minimum acceptable height. But a step on the scales showed I was a stone under the required minimum weight. The Inspector who interviewed me said he was sorry but advised me to try again for acceptance at a teacher training college. My paternal grandparents lived two streets from St Peter's College Saltley and a friend told me it was a good college. I sent off an application for teacher training. I was called to interview on Friday 13th December 1963 – my nineteenth birthday.

On arrival at the college I was taken to a small office and asked to wait. Eventually I was called to the office of Tom Platten, the college Principal. His first question was: "Why had I chosen St. Peters?" I told him that the college was my first choice; had an excellent reputation and it came highly recommended by a former student. (I did not tell him I couldn't get accepted at any college the previous year and would gladly have gone anywhere this year.) The interview was soon over; I was told: "We will let you know"; and I went home. At no time did I meet any of the P.E. staff, undergo any tests or see the facilities. My application was to do Physical Education as my main subject with Mathematics as my subsidiary subject. To the college's credit, and my surprise, I was notified by letter the following week that I was being offered a place on the course for 1964-67. What a relief after the humiliating rejections the previous year: I accepted by return post.

On arrival and registration at the college in September 1964 I discovered that it was possible to change one's chosen course choices; so I dumped Maths for History. A decision I have never regretted. But in 36 years, since qualifying, I was never timetabled to teach History. (I did, however, teach Maths for most of my 26 years before retirement.)

I loved my time at Saltley, the friendships I made and the success I enjoyed in sport and physical activities. In athletics I established the college High Jump record of just over six feet, was awarded my Athletics Colours in 1965 and became Athletics Captain in 1967 and also captain of the Gymnastics Club 1966/7.

David's record high jump in 1965.

1967 Football 1st Team. David is on the back row, third from left.

In football I was a goalkeeper; eventually becoming 1st Team keeper in early 1967 when the regular goalkeeper John 'Mitch' Mitchell switched successfully to playing as a forward. On the 1967 Easter Soccer tour to Germany I played in all the three games against strong Army teams in Minden and Hanover. We won all three without conceding a goal: 12.0, 7.0, and 5.0.

In swimming I endeared myself with the swimming tutor Bill Middleton (also known as Blackjack) by passing my Bronze Lifesaving certificate early in my first year, and progressing to Lifesaving Examiner's awards and Amateur Swimming Association Advanced Teacher's Certificates. He treated me very favourably; some of my less successful swimming colleagues were not so fortunate. He judged you by "Have you got your Bronze?"

At college I had a motorbike and wore all the gear: crash helmet, goggles, scarf, leathers, gauntlets and boots. Every time I got togged out I was greeted by either Jim or Rog with the comment "You would never guess he's only got a push bike!"

David Hudson

Post-Saltley Experiences

The day after finishing at Saltley I started teaching at High Park School in Stourbridge. I did two weeks before the end of term: but my full time contract began from 1st September 1967. I had been encouraged to apply for the post of 'Teacher of boys P.E.' by Bob Fletcher (Head of Maths at the school). He knew me by his sister Mary Cartwright who had taught with me at Edgecliff prior to me going to college. High Park was only four miles from my parents' home and looked a good opportunity. Bob said he would put in a good word for me to the headmaster Fred Stanier. But he knew the job required a second timetabled subject, and the school needed someone to teach technical drawing. At interview, therefore, I admitted I had done technical drawing a bit at secondary school and could sharpen a pencil. Job done: I was appointed. And I remained happily at High Park, and as it was transformed into Ridgewood High School, for the next 37 years before retirement.

Little did I know on leaving college that I would never again compete in the High Jump. There were no athletic clubs offering me opportunities for competition within 20 miles of my home in Kinver. But I could still impress my pupils by clearing nearly six feet using the straddle technique and landing on my back in the sand-filled school landing pit. However, in 1968, the world of high jumping changed forever. Dick Fosbury had won the Olympics in Mexico with the 'Fosbury Flop' with a leap of over seven feet and four inches. The Flop, according to one journalist, 'looked like a guy falling off the back of a truck.' Instead of the traditional straddle forward kick over the bar, it featured a mid-air rotation so that the jumper landed back-of-the-head-first on the mat. The new laws of high jumping allowed the jumpers head to lead the body; and to land safely on raised safety mattresses was a major incentive. High jumping entered a new era. (Since 1980 the world record has been held by jumpers using the Fosbury Flop.)

On reflection, I was envious of the new high jumping technique. I realised I could have vastly increased my own performance if I had known of it previously. But I also knew, if my own athletics competitive days were over, I could still coach, encourage and inspire my pupils towards sporting success and enjoyment in athletics, swimming, team sports, outdoor activities and other sporting activities. For the next ten years I was heavily involved in organising and developing football, athletics, swimming and life saving in the local district of Stourbridge and Halesowen. In outdoor activities I gained my Mountain Leadership Certificate and regularly instructed at Worcestershire's outdoor activities centre in Llanrug, Snowdonia. I particularly enjoyed instructing rock climbing in this area.

In football and cricket I played for local teams. I resisted offers to play football at higher levels due to my commitment and management of school and district teams. I especially enjoyed playing in the Birmingham Works League as goalkeeper and a guest player for Weldall and Assembly. (Works teams could have 2/3 players not employed by the company. The playing grounds were often brilliant and the quality of play outstanding. Several teams had former professional players in their twilight years playing for them.) I vividly remember the last match of my 'serious' football career: I was 35 years old and playing in goal for Kinver Reserves away at Clee Hill, Shropshire. This was a wild windswept area, it was poring with rain, bitterly cold and the pitch had just been cleared of sheep. My goalposts had no nets. The penalty area was very muddy with sparse grass but liberally manured by the departed sheep. The one lone spectator and his dog did not stay long. They missed the pathetic excuse for a game of football that followed. We lost. My thoughts became clear: 'What am I doing here?' I decided to hang up my boots.

I also decided that I was tired of having wet socks and kit teaching P.E. The extra hours after school, with matches and practices, and the evening management of the school's new sports hall was becoming exhausting. I was seeing too little of my wife Lynn and our two young children: Nigel and Emma★. My headmaster, Fred Stanier, agreed to me switching to teach Maths full time but also taking on pastoral responsibilities for pupils' welfare. In the mid-eighties I was granted a year's secondment to Birmingham University to study for a B.Phil Ed. degree in learning difficulties. On completion I returned to High Park in charge of remedial education and boy's welfare.

Both of my children pursued careers in education. Nigel chose the corporate route, training more than 4,000 people in marketing and business development before taking global responsibility for professional skills development at telecoms giant Vodafone. Today, in addition to his business and public speaking commitments, he's a doctoral researcher in workplace learning at the University of Chester Business School. Emma trained as a teacher. She spent ten years teaching primary school pupils in Stourbridge before I encouraged her to apply for a lectureship in Primary Education at Wolverhampton University. She applied successfully and was appointed as a Senior Lecturer. Lynn also sought to inspire people, spending over 30 years as a Church of England Lay Reader, loyally serving our local church and the Lichfield Diocese, before hanging up her cassock in favour of a quiet retirement.

My school was reorganised in 1990 by the local authority, merging with neighbouring school Longlands Secondary to become Ridgewood High School. Responsibilities were reallocated and I was appointed Head of Lower School, teaching

Maths and P.S.E. (Personal and Social Education). I was also designated Child Protection Officer for the school. I regularly attended case conferences with professionals from other agencies; social services, fostering, police, legal advisers, LEA reps, etc. and parents/guardians of the child, who were invited but did not always attend. It was not unusual for me to be the only professional present who had regular contact with the child. I have always admired the courage, honesty and determination of abused children to speak out and seek help. Too often, to my disgust, there were parental and family denials, poor follow up from social services and cursory police investigations leading to the child being ostracised, removed from the family home and put in care with no prosecution of the offending adults. Where is the justice in that for an innocent and trusting child when they bravely speak the truth and adults lie?

In the following years I was acting Deputy Head twice and finished, before granted early retirement in 2004, as Assistant Head teacher. (I shall never forget my interview by the LEA's doctor who had been asked to question my reasons for seeking early retirement. I was stunned by his opening question: "I have been asked to ascertain if you are likely to have an early death!" I don't know what he reported – I'm still going strong at 74 – but I was granted retirement at 60.)

I have been privileged to teach hundreds, possibly thousands, of lovely pupils and to support their development with their parents/guardians. It is still humbling to meet them locally and to remember wonderful times. I recently met a woman at my local supermarket who I recognised as a former pupil. She approached me and said "You must be Mr Hudson, your father taught me at High Park." Either I had remained with youthful looks or she needed to go to the opticians. Perhaps it's by maintaining one's interests in retirement that keeps us young?

David Hudson

When I stopped playing football, I joined Kinver Bowling Club. I am now the longest serving member. I have seen the club expand and been privileged to be Captain of its teams and Chairman of the club in recent years. My name appears on many club trophies.

Fishing and especially fly-fishing for trout has been one of my life's passions. In the 1970s I learnt how to tie artificial flies. One of the flies I developed – The Sedgetastic – has accounted for 90% of the fish I have caught. It has also become successful for many other anglers. In the last two years I have rediscovered an earlier love of coarse fishing for carp on a local lake that I previously managed in the 80s. I know huge carp live there. Hopefully, while I still have my strength, I can land one.

The only GCE exam I ever failed was O-level art in 1962. With a pencil or pen I could draw well from a model, photo or still life in front of me but struggled with compositions and painting pictures from memory. Also, as my art teacher recorded in a school report – 'Hudson has no sense of colour.' It is ironic, therefore, how much success I have enjoyed with commissioned paintings since retiring from teaching. I firmly believe you can learn how to paint and draw. I am largely self-taught by reading art books and magazines, watching instructional DVDs, attending a few one-day courses with brilliant artists, and by hours of practice. I now specialise in pastel portraits, pen and wash landscapes, caricatures and cartoons.

I have especially enjoyed teaching and encouraging a local art group. I am constantly amazed by their individual talents, humour and support for each other. They are lovely people.

**The spirit of Saltley College lives on:
"If you believe, you can do it!"**

www.ingramcontent.com/pod-product-compliance
Lightning Source LLC
Chambersburg PA
CBHW061744290426
43661CB00128B/1041